Edison vs. Tesla_ Electrical Battles

Edison vs. Tesla_ Electrical Battles

Rafeal Mechlore

UNIEK ENTERPRISES

CONTENTS

INDEX

Introduction:

1. Setting the stage for the electrifying rivalry between Thomas Edison and Nikola Tesla.
2. Brief overview of the historical and technological context in the late 19th and early 20th centuries.
3. Highlighting the immense impact of their contributions to electrical engineering.

INTRODUCTION

In the archives of logical history, barely any competitions have caught the public creative mind very like the awe-inspiring clash between two visionaries of the late nineteenth and mid twentieth hundreds of years: Thomas Edison and Nikola Tesla. This titanic conflict of brains and belief systems, frequently alluded to as the "Battle of Flows," denoted a basic point in the quick development of electrical innovation and power circulation. It was a fight not just for matchless quality in the arising electrical industry yet additionally for the actual eventual fate of current progress itself.

Thomas Alva Edison, the "Wizard of Menlo Park," was a productive American designer and business person. He held north of 1,000 licenses and was broadly viewed as the world's driving electrical trailblazer during his time. Edison's spearheading work in the advancement of direct flow (DC) electrical frameworks procured him colossal abundance and acclaim, and his creations enlightened urban communities, controlled ventures, and had an impact on the manner in which individuals lived.

Nikola Tesla, then again, was a Serbian-conceived designer and physicist who came to the US with a dream of a world fueled by substituting current (AC). Tesla's virtuoso lay in his extraordinary thoughts and creative AC framework, which guaranteed more effective, significant distance power transmission than Edison's DC framework. His commitments to the advancement of AC power would establish the groundwork for the cutting edge electrical matrix and carry power to homes and organizations all over the planet.

The contention among Edison and Tesla was not just a challenge of specialized ability, but rather likewise a conflict of differentiating ways of thinking, business procedures, and individual qualities. Edison was the epitome of the American pioneering soul, with an emphasis on common sense and attractiveness. Tesla, then again, was a visionary, driven by an energy for logical revelation and a craving to work on the human condition. Their disparities would fuel quite possibly of the most warmed and persuasive logical competition ever.

This story investigates the complex fight among Edison and Tesla, digging into the core of their advancements, the techniques they utilized, and the outcomes of their activities. It looks at how their contention at last formed the course of electrical designing, the energy business, and the cutting edge world. Past the specialized and business perspectives, their competition likewise features more extensive subjects of development, licensed innovation, and the exchange among science and trade.

In the accompanying pages, we will leave on an excursion through time, following the beginnings of Edison and Tesla's vocations, their separate commitments to electrical innovation, and the sensational showdowns that characterized their contention. We will investigate the key occasions, creations, and debates that obvious this phenomenal section throughout the entire existence of science and innovation. As we do as such, we will acquire understanding into the significant and enduring effect of their work, as well as the getting through tradition of the electrical fights that set Edison in opposition to Tesla.

1. **Setting the stage for the electrifying rivalry between Thomas Edison and Nikola Tesla.**

   The late nineteenth century was a period of momentous mechanical headway, and barely any areas of development held as much commitment and interest as the field of power. It was against this background of thriving logical revelation and modern change that the zapping competition between two splendid personalities, Thomas Edison and Nikola Tesla, became the dominant focal point. To completely see the value in the amazing fight that would unfurl, it's fundamental to figure out the specific circumstance, the characters, and the emotional setting that set up for their conflict.

   The Beginning of the Electrical Age

   At the beginning of the electrical age in the last part of the 1800s, the world was going through a significant change. The Modern Unrest was going full speed ahead, introducing a time of exceptional advancement and urbanization. Urban communities were developing quickly, and the interest for a dependable and proficient wellspring of force was central. This request set out a freedom for designers and business people like Edison and Tesla to shape what's to come.

   Thomas Edison: The American Trend-setter

   Thomas Edison, an American creator and business visionary, was at that point an easily recognized name when the electrical competition started. Brought into the world in 1847 in Milan, Ohio, Edison was an independent man with a resolute hard working attitude and an unquenchable interest. His initial developments, for example, the phonograph and the glowing light, had previously gotten his standing as a splendid pioneer.

   Edison's excursion into the universe of power started when he laid out his research center in Menlo Park, New Jersey, frequently alluded to as the "creation manufacturing plant." It was here that he would make the foundation for orderly creation and take huge steps in the improvement of electrical innovation.

One of Edison's vital commitments to the electrical scene was the flawlessness of the brilliant light. While others had made renditions of the light before him, Edison's variant was the primary commonsense and economically practical model. It denoted the start of an upset in metropolitan lighting, as urban communities across the US and all over the planet started to embrace electric lighting frameworks.

The Introduction of Direct Current (DC)

Edison's vision for electrical appropriation depended on direct flow (DC) innovation. In a DC framework, electrical flow streams constantly in one bearing from a power source to the buyer. Edison accepted that DC was more secure as well as more viable for the charge of urban communities. He started constructing DC power stations and circulation organizations, making power accessible to the majority.

In any case, there was a huge constraint to Edison's DC framework: it experienced transmission misfortunes over significant distances. The electrical energy would lessen as it voyaged, making it unrealistic for controlling urban communities arranged a long way from the power age source. This restriction would ultimately carry Edison into direct clash with an alternate opponent way to deal with electrical circulation.

Nikola Tesla: The Visionary

Nikola Tesla, brought into the world in 1856 in Smiljan, Croatia (then, at that point, a piece of the Austrian Realm), was a visionary with a capricious brain. Since early on, he exhibited a remarkable fitness for math and physical science. He emigrated to the US in 1884, showing up in New York City with minimal in excess of a fantasy and a letter of proposal from Charles Batchelor, an Edison representative who perceived Tesla's splendor.

Tesla was a man of transcending desire. His objective was completely reforming the world's electrical frameworks, and he trusted that substituting flow (AC) was the key. Dissimilar to DC, AC power occasionally heads in a different path, a property that Tesla considered to be favorable for significant distance transmission. He immediately protected work with Edison yet wound up in conflict with his manager over the eventual fate of electrical circulation.

The Air conditioner versus DC Fight

The stage was set for a standoff between these two noteworthy innovators. Edison was a resolute backer of DC, while Tesla supported the reason for AC. Their disparities reached out past simple specialized inclinations; they addressed two generally dissimilar methods of reasoning.

Edison, the viable business person, zeroed in on steady enhancements and tried to carry power to the majority through confined DC appropriation organizations. He was likewise a defender of the hot seat, which utilized DC to execute hoodlums, and involved this as a show of its alleged security.

Tesla, the visionary, imagined an existence where power could be communicated over tremendous distances proficiently and securely utilizing AC. He accepted that air conditioner was the unrivaled decision for power transmission as well as the way to opening the maximum capacity of power as a widespread utility.

Enter George Westinghouse

The fight among Edison and Tesla over AC versus DC would raise when George Westinghouse, an American business visionary and creator, entered the scene. Westinghouse perceived the capability of AC innovation and cooperated with Tesla to advance its utilization. The Westinghouse Electric Organization turned into Edison's essential rival in the competition to charge America.

One of the essential minutes in the contention happened during the "Battle of Flows." Edison sent off a slanderous attack against AC, looking to depict it as perilous and questionable, in any event, going similarly as freely shocking creatures with AC flow to exhibit its alleged risks. Tesla and Westinghouse, then again, centered around the effectiveness and wellbeing of AC transmission.

The Fight for the World's Fair

The 1893 World's Columbian Piece in Chicago turned into a landmark for the air conditioner versus DC contention. Both Westinghouse and General Electric (Edison's organization) went after the agreement to charge the fair. Edison's group proposed a monstrous DC framework, while Westinghouse and Tesla pushed for AC.

Eventually, Westinghouse won the agreement, and the fair was enlightened by the splendor of AC power. This triumph was a critical defining moment in the fight for popular assessment and denoted the start of AC's domination in the electrical business.

The Consequence

The zapping contention among Edison and Tesla at last came to a nearby, however the tradition of their commitments to electrical designing persevered. Tesla's AC framework would proceed to rule power transmission, permitting power to proficiently be communicated over significant distances. This prepared for the development of monstrous power plants, which could give power to whole urban communities from a solitary source. Edison's DC framework, while losing the fight for power transmission, tracked down its specialty in nearby dissemination and certain particular applications.

In 1897, Tesla's rotating current framework was chosen for the amazing Niagara Falls power project, further establishing the triumph of AC over DC for significant distance power transmission. This undertaking would exhibit the possibility and effectiveness of Tesla's AC innovation on an excellent scale, conveying power to Bison, New York, and preparing for the broad reception of AC power frameworks around the world.

2. **Brief overview of the historical and technological context in the late 19th and early 20th centuries.**

To genuinely comprehend the zapping competition between Thomas Edison and Nikola Tesla, we should dive into the verifiable and mechanical setting of the late nineteenth and mid twentieth hundreds of years. This period was set apart by wonderful headways, wild change, and a hunger for development that would make way for perhaps of the most notorious logical contention ever. In this outline, we will investigate the setting against which Edison and Tesla's commitments unfurled, enveloping everything from the Modern Upheaval to the beginning of the electrical age, the development of urbanization, and the more extensive social and monetary changes of the period.

The Modern Upset: An Impetus for Change

The late nineteenth century was profoundly affected by the continuous impacts of the Modern Upheaval, which had started in the late eighteenth hundred years. The Modern Transformation changed society by presenting motorization, urbanization, and new methods of creation. This period saw the shift from agrarian economies to modern and assembling based social orders, igniting a remarkable rush of advancement and financial development.

The automation of farming and the advancement of material production lines were among the early impetuses of the Modern Upset. This prompted expanded farming efficiency and an overflow of work, which, thus, powered urbanization as individuals relocated from rustic regions to urban communities looking for business open doors in thriving production lines.

Urbanization: The Ascent of the Cutting edge City

Urbanization was a characterizing component of the late nineteenth hundred years. Urban areas extended quickly as individuals ran to metropolitan focuses looking for work and better day to day environments. This mass movement to urban communities was worked with by further developed transportation organizations, for example, rail routes, which associated rustic regions to metro-politan centers.

The development of urban areas represented various difficulties, including stuffing, lacking lodging, and sterilization issues. In any case, it additionally set out open doors for development and mechanical progression. Urban areas became center points of

industry, trade, and social trade, making way for the advancement of present day foundation and administrations.

The Development of Industry

The development of industry during this period was completely extraordinary. New innovations and assembling processes altered creation techniques, prompting expanded effectiveness and the large scale manufacturing of merchandise. Developments, for example, the Bessemer cycle for steel creation and the mechanical production system methods spearheaded by Henry Passage in the mid twentieth century exemplified the industrialization of assembling.

Production lines jumped up across industrialized countries, controlled by steam motors and, later, power. This shift from physical work to motorization supported efficiency as well as laid the foundation for the broad reception of electrical power.

The Introduction of the Electrical Age

In the midst of the fast industrialization and urbanization of the late nineteenth 100 years, power arose as a progressive power with the possibility to change each part of society. The bridling and dispersion of power vowed to give a spotless, proficient, and flexible wellspring of force, upsetting businesses, transportation, and, surprisingly, day to day existence.

Power was viewed for the purpose of progress, with applications going from lighting roads and homes to driving manufacturing plants and transportation frameworks. Obviously the improvement of electrical innovation would assume a urgent part in forming what's to come.

The Trailblazers of Electrical Advancement: Edison and Tesla

At the core of the jolt development were two splendid designers: Thomas Edison and Nikola Tesla. Each brought a novel arrangement of abilities, viewpoints, and developments to the table, and their competition would be instrumental in characterizing the direction of electrical designing and power circulation.

Thomas Edison: The Wizard of Menlo Park

Thomas Alva Edison, brought into the world in 1847, was the encapsulation of the American soul of advancement and business. With a determined hard working attitude and an unquenchable interest, Edison became perhaps of the most productive designer ever. His commitments reached out a long ways past power and included developments, for example, the phonograph and the film camera.

Edison's excursion into the universe of power started with his foundation of the Menlo Park research facility in New Jersey, frequently alluded to as the "development processing plant." Here, he established a climate for precise creation and took critical steps in electrical innovation. One of his most well known developments was the brilliant light, which denoted a defining moment in metropolitan lighting and set up for broad charge.

Nikola Tesla: The Visionary Virtuoso

Nikola Tesla, brought into the world in 1856 in Croatia (then, at that point, a piece of the Austrian Realm), was a visionary virtuoso with a propensity for imaginative reasoning. Since early on, Tesla exhibited an uncommon inclination for science and physical science. He emigrated to the US in 1884, showing up in New York City with minimal in excess of a fantasy and a letter of proposal from Charles Batchelor, an Edison worker who perceived Tesla's brightness.

Tesla's vision for the fate of power depended on rotating current (AC). In contrast to coordinate flow (DC), which Edison advocated, AC power occasionally takes an alternate route. Tesla accepted that air conditioner was the predominant decision for power transmission as well as the way to opening the maximum capacity of power as a widespread utility.

The Clash of Flows: AC versus DC

The charging competition among Edison and Tesla was in excess of a conflict of specialized inclinations; it was a showdown of belief systems and business techniques. Edison pushed for DC, which streamed persistently in one bearing, while Tesla advocated AC for its capacity to send control over significant distances productively.

Edison accepted that DC was more secure and more reasonable for confined dissemination, while Tesla considered AC to be the eventual fate of significant distance power transmission. Their disparities reached out past specialized matters, as Edison was a commonsense business person, while Tesla was a visionary.

George Westinghouse: The Third Player

The contention among Edison and Tesla arrived at its apex when George Westinghouse, an American business visionary and innovator, entered the scene. Perceiving the capability of Tesla's AC innovation, Westinghouse collaborated with him to advance AC power dissemination. The Westinghouse Electric Organization turned into Edison's essential rival in the competition to charge America.

One of the urgent minutes in the air conditioner versus DC fight happened during the "Battle of Flows." Edison sent off a slanderous attack against AC, endeavoring to depict it as risky and inconsistent. He even turned to freely shocking creatures with AC flow to

exhibit its alleged perils. Conversely, Tesla and Westinghouse zeroed in on the proficiency and wellbeing of AC transmission.

The Chicago World's Fair: A Defining moment

The 1893 World's Columbian Piece in Chicago turned into an essential milestone in the air conditioner versus DC competition. Both Westinghouse and General Electric (Edison's organization) competed for the agreement to charge the fair. Edison's group proposed an enormous DC framework, while Westinghouse and Tesla pushed for AC.

Westinghouse won the agreement, and the fair was enlightened by the brightness of AC power. This triumph not just exhibited the productivity and security of AC yet in addition denoted a critical defining moment in the fight for popular assessment.

The Niagara Falls Venture: AC Wins

In 1897, Tesla's AC framework was chosen for the stupendous Niagara Falls power project, further establishing the triumph of AC over DC for significant distance power transmission. This venture showed the practicality and productivity of Tesla's AC innovation on an excellent scale, conveying power to Bison, New York, and preparing for the inescapable reception of AC power frameworks around the world.

3. **Highlighting the immense impact of their contributions to electrical engineering.**

The late nineteenth and mid twentieth hundreds of years saw an upset in the field of electrical designing, and at the front of this extraordinary period were two splendid personalities — Thomas Edison and Nikola Tesla. Their weighty creations, visionary thoughts, and constant quest for logical development always impacted the world. In this complete investigation, we will dig into the colossal effect of their commitments to electrical designing, looking at their creations, frameworks, and enduring heritages that keep on forming our cutting edge world.

Thomas Edison: The "Wizard of Menlo Park"

Thomas Alva Edison, brought into the world in 1847, was an American creator, business visionary, and light of electrical designing. His vocation spread over a striking time of innovative headway, and Edison's work contacted essentially every feature of electrical designing.

1. **The Radiant Light**

   Edison's most notable creation was without a doubt the brilliant light. Before his leap forward, fake lighting was faint, inconsistent, and frequently risky. In 1879, Edison effectively showed a reasonable, enduring, and economically feasible brilliant light. His

   bulb utilized a carbonized bamboo fiber, which sparkled splendidly when an electric flow went through it. This creation changed society by enlightening homes, roads, and organizations, accordingly upgrading security and efficiency. The effect of the glowing light reached out past lighting; it generally changed the manner in which individuals lived and worked. Urban communities that once slept in haziness woke up around evening time, empowering longer work hours, new types of diversion, and improved personal satisfaction.

2. **The Electrical Power Framework**

   Edison's momentous work was not restricted to the light; he fostered a whole electrical power framework to go with it. His immediate flow (DC) framework included the consistent progression of electrical charge in one course. In 1882, Edison introduced the world's most memorable business electric power station in New York City, denoting the start of metropolitan charge.

   In spite of the fact that Edison's DC framework had restrictions, for example, energy misfortune over significant distances, it laid the preparation for unified influence age and circulation organizations. His attention on reasonableness and his accentuation on wellbeing contributed fundamentally to the development of electrical designing.

3. **The Phonograph**

   In 1877, Edison disclosed another notable development — the phonograph. This gadget could record and repeat sound, changing the universe of sound diversion. Edison's phonograph established the groundwork for the advanced music industry, taking into consideration the large scale manufacturing and appropriation of recorded music. It addressed a fantastic jump in the field of electrical designing and sound innovation.

4. **The Movie Camera**

Edison's advancements stretched out into the domain of films with the formation of the kinetoscope, a movie camera created in the late nineteenth 100 years. This innovation denoted the beginning of film, making way for the cutting edge entertainment world. Edison's commitments to amusement and correspondence have done great things.

Nikola Tesla: The Visionary Virtuoso

As a conspicuous difference to Edison's common sense, Nikola Tesla, brought into the world in 1856, was a visionary virtuoso whose creative thoughts changed electrical designing. His creative ideas established the groundwork for current power dissemination frameworks, remote correspondence, and various mechanical headways.

1. **AC Power Transmission**

   Tesla's most huge commitment to electrical designing was the advancement of the exchanging flow (AC) power framework. In contrast to coordinate current (DC), AC occasionally takes an alternate route, considering productive significant distance power transmission. Tesla's AC innovation tended to the limits of DC, like energy misfortune overstretched distances.

   In 1891, Tesla licensed the "Tesla loop," a crucial part in AC power conveyance frameworks. His work in AC power transmission shaped the reason for the development of gigantic power plants fit for providing power to whole areas. Tesla's AC framework upset electrical designing, making significant distance power transmission plausible and proficient.

2. **The Enlistment Engine**

   Tesla's creation of the air conditioner enlistment engine was a unique advantage for electrical designing. The Air conditioner engine was more proficient and flexible than its DC partner, making it reasonable for many applications. It controlled modern apparatus, domestic devices, and different gadgets, adding to the zap of homes and manufacturing plants.

   The Air conditioner enlistment engine's effect was significant, as it assumed a pivotal part in the industrialization and motorization of various cycles, from assembling to transportation.

3. **Remote Correspondence**

Tesla's visionary reasoning stretched out to the domain of remote correspondence. He explored different avenues regarding the transmission of electromagnetic waves through the earth and the air, expecting the standards of remote correspondence that would later empower radio, TV, and present day media communications.

Tesla's spearheading work in remote correspondence established the groundwork for the advancement of radio and other remote advances. His visionary ideas keep on affecting broadcast communications and the remote business today.

4. **The Tesla Curl and High-Recurrence Exchanging Current**

Tesla's work with high-recurrence exchanging flow and the Tesla curl had broad ramifications for electrical designing. His creations in this domain added to the improvement of remote power transmission, high-recurrence radio transmission, and, surprisingly, early X-beam innovation.

The Tesla loop, specifically, turned into a fundamental apparatus in exploration and trial and error in the field of electrical designing. Its capacity to produce very high voltages

and make astounding electrical presentations captivated researchers and creators, impacting resulting improvements in the field.

Influence on Electrical Designing

The commitments of Edison and Tesla to electrical designing enduringly affect the field. Their advancements have formed the development of electrical frameworks, power age, and correspondence innovations. Here are a few key regions where their impact is generally articulated:

1. **Headway of Electrical Power Age and Conveyance**

Edison's advancement of the DC power framework and Tesla's spearheading work in AC power transmission on a very basic level changed electrical power age and dispersion. Edison's functional methodology laid out the idea of concentrated power age, while Tesla's AC framework reformed significant distance power transmission.

Today, the world depends overwhelmingly on AC power transmission for its productivity and flexibility. Tesla's visionary thoughts laid the foundation for the development of huge power plants, giving power to whole locales and empowering the charge of urban communities on an excellent scale. Edison's accentuation on security and reasonableness likewise added to the improvement of normalized electrical frameworks and wellbeing conventions.

2. **Jolt of Enterprises and Urbanization**

   The jolt of enterprises and metropolitan focuses during the late nineteenth and mid twentieth hundreds of years was intently attached to the commitments of Edison and Tesla. Edison's brilliant light and electrical power framework changed plants, workplaces, and homes, improving security and efficiency. Tesla's AC enlistment engine controlled modern apparatus and considered the inescapable reception of electrically determined gear.

   The development of urbanization during this period was worked with by the accessibility of electric lighting and power. Edison's reasonable advancements pulled in individuals to urban communities, where they could profit from the accommodations of electrical innovation. Tesla's AC framework, with its productivity and limit with regards to significant distance power transmission, assumed a vital part in the zap of metropolitan regions.

3. **Amusement and Correspondence Transformation**

   Edison's developments, for example, the phonograph and the film camera, altered media outlets. These developments established the groundwork for the cutting edge

   music and entertainment worlds, reshaping the manner in which individuals consumed culture and amusement.

   Tesla's visionary work in remote correspondence and high-recurrence rotating current set up for the advancement of radio and broadcast communications. His ground breaking ideas expected the remote advancements that would associate individuals across the globe, from early radio stations to current cell phones and the web.

4. **Heritage in Exploration and Advancement**

Past their particular creations, Edison and Tesla left getting through heritages in exploration and advancement. Edison's orderly way to deal with development and constant trial and error turned into a model for future creators and specialists. His accentuation on reasonableness and business practicality keeps on impacting the fields of designing and innovation.

Tesla's visionary reasoning and readiness to investigate eccentric thoughts have enlivened researchers and innovators for ages. His work on remote correspondence, high-recurrence power, and electromagnetic waves established the groundwork for critical mechanical headways in the twentieth and 21st hundreds of years.

1 |

Chapter 1

The Pioneers of Electricity

Power, the basic power of nature that drives our cutting edge world, has a rich history of investigation, trial and error, and development. From its earliest revelation as electricity produced via friction to the improvement of mind boggling electrical frameworks that light our homes and power our businesses, the trailblazers of power have made a permanent imprint on human civilization. In this far reaching investigation, we will leave on an excursion through the lives and commitments of these electrical visionaries, following the development of power from its baffling beginnings to the current day.

Old Miracles and the Introduction of Electrical Information

1.1 The Beginnings of Electrical Peculiarities

The excursion of power starts in ancient history, where the perception of normal electrical peculiarities, like lightning and friction based electricity, ignited interest and interest. Old civilizations, including the Greeks and Egyptians, recorded their perceptions of these baffling powers. Stories of the legendary golden stone and its capacity to draw in objects through static charge laid the basis for later logical request.

1.2 The Early Trailblazers

As human comprehension of power gradually progressed, remarkable figures like Thales of Miletus and William Gilbert made critical commitments to the field. Thales, a Greek rationalist, was among quick to report the zapping properties of golden around 600 BCE. Gilbert, an English researcher in the sixteenth 100 years, led broad tests on magnets and power, begetting the expression "power" and establishing the groundwork for future exploration.

The Illumination and the Period of Revelation

2.1 The Leyden Container and Early Capacitors

The eighteenth century saw a flood in electrical investigation during the Edification. One of the most vital creations of this period was the Leyden container, a forerunner to the cutting edge capacitor. Ewald Georg von Kleist and Pieter van Musschenbroek, autonomously fostered the Leyden container during the 1740s. This gadget could store

electrical charge and release it in a controlled way, preparing for the investigation of electric potential and energy stockpiling.

2.2 Benjamin Franklin and His Analyses

Benjamin Franklin, one of the Initial architects of the US, had a significant effect on the investigation of power during the eighteenth hundred years. His well known kite analyze in 1752 showed the electrical idea of lightning and added to the comprehension of electrical conductivity. Franklin's work with lightning poles likewise progressed the reasonable uses of power by shielding structures from lightning strikes.

The Beginning of Electric Circuits and Attraction

3.1 Alessandro Volta and the Development of the Battery

The late eighteenth and mid nineteenth hundreds of years denoted a time of huge development in power. Italian researcher Alessandro Volta, in 1800, acquainted the world with the primary synthetic battery, known as the Voltaic Heap. This creation exhibited the chance of producing a constant progression of power, prompting the improvement of electric circuits. The unit of electrical potential, the volt, is named in his honor.

3.2 Hans Christian Ørsted and the Revelation of Electromagnetism

In 1820, Danish physicist Hans Christian Ørsted made an earth shattering disclosure that connected power and attraction. Through his tests, Ørsted saw that an electric flow moving through a wire could redirect a close by attractive needle. This disclosure established the groundwork for the investigation of electromagnetism, a field that would later prompt the improvement of electric engines and generators.

Michael Faraday and the Laws of Electromagnetic Enlistment

4.1 Michael Faraday: The Dad of Electromagnetic Acceptance

Perhaps of the most powerful figure throughout the entire existence of power is Michael Faraday, a self-trained English researcher. During the 1830s, Faraday led notable tests on electromagnetic enlistment. His work showed the way that a changing attractive field could prompt an electric flow in a close by channel. Faraday's trials prompted the definition of Faraday's Laws of Electromagnetic Acceptance, which support the activity of generators and transformers.

4.2 Faraday's Commitment to Electrochemistry

Notwithstanding his work on electromagnetic acceptance, Faraday made critical commitments to electrochemistry. He presented the idea of electric and compound potential, which prompted the improvement of electrochemical cells and batteries.

Faraday's experiences made ready for pragmatic utilizations of power in fields like electroplating and electrochemical examination.

The Introduction of the Message and the Electric Telecommunication Insurgency

5.1 Samuel Morse and the Morse Code

The nineteenth century saw an upset in significant distance correspondence with the development of the message. American designer Samuel Morse, in a joint effort with others like Alfred Vail, fostered the Morse code — an arrangement of specks and runs addressing letters and numbers. The message, controlled by power, permitted messages to be sent rapidly over immense distances, it was conveyed to change the way data.

5.2 The Message's Effect on Society and Business

The message significantly affected society, business, and the dispersal of information. It worked with fast correspondence between far off areas, empowering the coordination of transportation, exchange, and monetary exchanges. The "wired world" made by the message laid the basis for the worldwide correspondence organizations representing things to come.

Influence, the fundamental influence of nature that drives our state of the art world, has a rich history of examination, experimentation, and improvement. From its earliest disclosure as power delivered by means of contact to the improvement of marvelous electrical structures that light our homes and power our organizations, the pioneers of force have made a long-lasting engraving on human progress. In this expansive examination, we will leave on a journey through the lives and responsibilities of these electrical visionaries, following the advancement of force from its bewildering starting points to the flow day.

Old Supernatural occurrences and the Presentation of Electrical Data

1.1 The Starting points of Electrical Quirks

The journey of force begins in old history, where the impression of typical electrical quirks, such as lightning and rubbing based power, touched off endlessly interest. Old human advancements, including the Greeks and Egyptians, recorded their impression of these astounding powers. Accounts of the unbelievable brilliant stone and its ability to attract objects through static charge laid the reason for later consistent solicitation.

1.2 The Early Pioneers

As human cognizance of force step by step advanced, momentous figures like Thales of Miletus and William Gilbert committed to the field. Thales, a Greek pragmatist, rushed to report the destroying properties of brilliant around 600 BCE. Gilbert, an English scientist in the sixteenth 100 years, drove expansive tests on magnets and power, generating the saying "power" and laying out the basis for future investigation.

The Light and the Time of Disclosure

2.1 The Leyden Holder and Early Capacitors

The eighteenth century saw a flood in electrical examination during the Illumination. One of the most fundamental manifestations of this period was the Leyden holder, a trailblazer to the state of the art capacitor. Ewald Georg von Kleist and Pieter van Musschenbroek, independently encouraged the Leyden compartment during the 1740s. This device could store electrical charge and delivery it in a controlled manner, getting ready for the examination of electric potential and energy amassing.

2.2 Benjamin Franklin and His Examinations

Benjamin Franklin, one of the Underlying engineers of the US, fundamentally affected the examination of force during the eighteenth hundred years. His notable kite examine in 1752 showed the electrical thought of lightning and added to the perception of electrical conductivity. Franklin's work with lightning posts in like manner advanced the sensible purposes of force by protecting designs from lightning strikes.

The Start of Electric Circuits and Fascination

3.1 Alessandro Volta and the Improvement of the Battery

The late eighteenth and mid nineteenth many years meant a period of immense improvement in power. Italian scientist Alessandro Volta, in 1800, familiar the world with the essential manufactured battery, known as the Voltaic Pile. This creation showed the possibility delivering a steady movement of force, inciting the improvement of electric circuits. The unit of electrical potential, the volt, is named in his honor.

3.2 Hans Christian Ørsted and the Disclosure of Electromagnetism

In 1820, Danish physicist Hans Christian Ørsted made a momentous exposure that associated power and fascination. Through his tests, Ørsted saw that an electric stream traveling through a wire could divert a nearby alluring needle. This divulgence laid out the preparation for the examination of electromagnetism, a field that would later incite the improvement of electric motors and generators.

Michael Faraday and the Laws of Electromagnetic Enrollment

4.1 Michael Faraday: The Father of Electromagnetic Acknowledgment

Maybe of the most remarkable figure all through the whole presence of force is Michael Faraday, a self-prepared English specialist. During the 1830s, Faraday drove eminent tests on electromagnetic enrollment. His work showed the way that a changing

appealing field could provoke an electric stream in a nearby channel. Faraday's preliminaries incited the meaning of Faraday's Laws of Electromagnetic Acknowledgment, which support the action of generators and transformers.

4.2 Faraday's Obligation to Electrochemistry

Despite his work on electromagnetic acknowledgment, Faraday genuinely committed to electrochemistry. He introduced the possibility of electric and compound potential, which provoked the improvement of electrochemical cells and batteries. Faraday's encounters prepared for logical uses of force in fields like electroplating and electrochemical assessment.

The Presentation of the Message and the Electric Telecom Insurrection

5.1 Samuel Morse and the Morse Code

The nineteenth century saw an agitated in huge distance correspondence with the advancement of the message. American planner Samuel Morse, in a joint exertion with others like Alfred Vail, cultivated the Morse code — a course of action of spots and runs tending to letters and numbers. The message, constrained by power, allowed messages to be sent quickly over gigantic distances, significantly altering how data was conveyed.

5.2 The Message's Impact on Society and Business

The message altogether impacted society, business, and the dispersal of data. It worked with quick correspondence between distant regions, engaging the coordination of transportation, trade, and money related trades. The "wired world" made by the message laid the reason for the overall correspondence associations addressing what might be on the horizon.

1.1 Introduction to Edison and Tesla as young inventors.

The tales of Thomas Edison and Nikola Tesla, two of the most notorious figures throughout the entire existence of electrical designing, are frequently connected with their earth shattering commitments to the field as grown-ups. Nonetheless, the seeds of their virtuoso and development were planted during their early stages as youthful innovators. In this investigation, we will dig into the early lives and encounters of Edison and Tesla, revealing insight into the occasions and impacts that molded their excursions from inquisitive adolescents to visionary designers.

Thomas Edison: The Youthful Hobbyist

Thomas Alva Edison, brought into the world on February 11, 1847, in Milan, Ohio, came from humble starting points. His initial years were set apart by a tireless interest and a

voracious hunger for information. Edison's excursion as a youthful designer started some time before he would turn into the "Wizard of Menlo Park."

1. **An Inquisitive Childhood**

   Edison's curiosity was obvious since early on. He was known for posing endless inquiries and leading little analyses in his experience growing up home. His mom, Nancy Edison, perceived his hunger for information and permitted him to change a side of their cellar into a shoddy lab, giving the youthful Edison a space to support his sprouting advantages.

2. **The Impact of Perusing and Self-Training**

   Edison's conventional training was restricted, with just three months of formal tutoring. Nonetheless, he was a devoted peruser and unquenchable student. He gobbled up books on a large number of subjects and was especially attracted to deals with science and designing. Edison's self-schooling assumed a critical part in molding his scholarly development and his possible way as a designer.

3. **Early Business and Telecommunication**

As a youngster, Edison displayed a sharp enterprising soul. At 12 years old, he started offering papers and candy to prepare travelers, procuring an unassuming pay. His initial introduction to the universe of telecommunication happened when he saved a kid from an approaching train, and the kid's thankful dad, a message administrator, showed Edison the essentials of telecommunication as a prize. This prologue to the message started Edison's interest with electrical correspondence.

4. **The Youthful Edison's Innovations**

Edison's initial examinations and creations incorporated various mechanical and electrical gadgets. One of his most memorable developments was a programmed vote recorder, intended to smooth out the method involved with counting votes in regulative gatherings. While the gadget was rarely generally taken on, it displayed Edison's talent for advancement and critical thinking.

Nikola Tesla: The Bright Virtuoso

Nikola Tesla, brought into the world on July 10, 1856, in Smiljan, Croatia (then piece of the Austrian Domain), was one more youthful creator whose early life alluded to the splendor that would later characterize his vocation. Tesla's excursion from a little town in Europe to turning into a prestigious electrical visionary was set apart by interest, assurance, and a significant comprehension of electrical peculiarities.

1. **Early Interest with Power**

As a kid, Tesla was enraptured by the normal world and,

specifically, by the force of power. He related clear recollections of seeing lightning storms and being struck by the sheer marvel and excellence of electrical releases. This interest with power would turn into a main impetus all through his life.

2. **Quest for Formal Training**

   Tesla's quest for formal schooling was set apart by a hunger for information and a steady obligation to his examinations. He went to the Genuine Recreation center in Karlovac, Croatia, where he succeeded in math and material science. His energy for electrical designing drove him to enlist at the Specialized College of Graz in Austria, where he concentrated on electrical designing.

3. **Early Work and Difficulties**

   After finishing his examinations, Tesla tracked down work as an electrical designer in different European urban areas. His initial vocation was set apart by difficulties and misfortunes, remembering challenges for getting solid job and confronting monetary difficulties. Nonetheless, these encounters would shape Tesla's versatility and assurance to prevail as an innovator.

4. **The Vision of Exchanging Current**

Tesla's profound comprehension of electrical peculiarities drove him to imagine the capability of exchanging flow (AC) as a prevalent method for power age and transmission. During his time working in Budapest and later in Paris, he started fostering his thoughts and ideas for AC frameworks. Tesla's energy for AC power would ultimately lead him to the US and into a pivotal experience with Thomas Edison.

1.2 Their early experiments with electricity and magnetic fields.

The excursions of Thomas Edison and Nikola Tesla as youthful creators were profoundly interwoven with their interest with power and attractive fields. In this investigation, we will dive into the early analyses and disclosures of Edison and Tesla in these areas, following the essential minutes that molded comprehension they might interpret electrical and attractive peculiarities and set up for their momentous commitments to science and designing.

Thomas Edison's Initial Investigations

Thomas Edison's interest with power started during his childhood in Milan, Ohio. His initial examinations and perceptions established the groundwork for his long lasting excursion as an innovator and electrical trailblazer.

1. **Electromagnetism and Telecommunication**

   First experience with the universe of power got through his work as a message administrator. At 15 years old, he started functioning as a telegrapher for the Fabulous Trunk Rail line in Port Huron, Michigan. This occupation permitted him to collaborate with broadcast gear, including electromagnets, batteries, and electrical circuits.

   One of Edison's initial tests included working on the proficiency of the message framework. He fostered a gadget that permitted transmit administrators to send various messages all the while on a solitary message wire — a critical progression in telecommunication. This examination denoted the start of his investigation of electrical and attractive fields.

2. **Edison's Most memorable Patent: The Electric Vote Recorder**

   In 1868, at 21 years old, Edison accepted his most memorable patent for the creation of an electric vote recorder. This gadget was intended to computerize the course of vote counting in administrative congregations, diminishing the potential for human blunder. While the electric vote recorder was not generally taken on, it showed Edison's initial interest in applying power to functional issues.

3. **The Stock Ticker and Electrical Advancements**

Edison's next critical endeavor was the advancement of a superior stock ticker for sending securities exchange data. This development earned respect and monetary achievement, furnishing Edison with the assets to lay out his own research facility in Menlo Park, New Jersey, where he would proceed to direct a large number of tests and creations.

Edison's initial analyses at Menlo Park remembered headways for telecommunication, phonography, and radiant lighting. His work on the carbon transmitter, a fundamental part of early phones, added to the improvement of voice correspondence.

Nikola Tesla's Initial Analyses

Nikola Tesla's interest with power and attractive fields started during his initial training in Europe. His inventive trials and visionary thoughts would eventually shape the fate of electrical designing.

1. **The Excursion to the US**

   Subsequent to concentrating on electrical designing in Europe and working for different electrical organizations, Tesla settled on an earth shattering choice to go to the US. In 1884, he showed up in New York City with minimal in excess of a letter of proposal and a brain loaded up with progressive thoughts regarding power.

2. **Exchanging Current and Enlistment Engines**

   Tesla's most critical early investigations spun around rotating current (AC) and the advancement of the air conditioner enlistment engine. In contrast to the immediate flow (DC) frameworks supported by Edison, Tesla saw the capability of AC for its capacity to communicate power over significant distances proficiently.

   One of Tesla's leading edge minutes happened while he was strolling in a recreation area in Budapest. He imagined the pivoting attractive field, a major idea that would prompt the improvement of the air conditioner enlistment engine. This development denoted a critical crossroads throughout the entire existence of electrical designing, as it considered the proficient transformation of electrical energy into mechanical work.

3. **Tesla's AC Polyphase Framework**

   Tesla's analyses with AC prompted the making of the polyphase substituting current framework. He fostered a bunch of conditions that depicted the way of behaving of polyphase frameworks, which included various AC waveforms with explicit stage connections. This framework established the groundwork for the proficient age, transmission, and dissemination of power for a huge scope.

4. **The Tesla Curl and High-Recurrence Substituting Current**
Tesla's work with the Tesla curl and high-recurrence rotating current (HFAC) was another earth shattering undertaking. The Tesla loop was equipped for producing incredibly high voltages and making dynamite electrical showcases. This creation would later turn into an essential device in exploration and trial and error, displaying Tesla's ability in working with power and attractive fields.

5. **Remote Transmission of Power**

One of Tesla's most nervy thoughts was the remote transmission of power. He accepted that it was feasible to communicate electrical power through the earth and the environment, imagining a reality where power could be conveyed without the requirement for wires. While his Wardenclyffe Pinnacle project planned to show remote power transmission, it was never completely acknowledged because of monetary imperatives.

Looking at Edison and Tesla's Initial Examinations

1. **Edison: Pragmatic Advancement**
Edison's initial tests were described by a sober minded way to deal with critical thinking. He looked for viable applications for power, especially in telecommunication and later in electric lighting. Edison's innovations were driven by a craving to work on existing frameworks and make them more proficient and open to the general population.

2. **Tesla: Visionary Ideas**

Tesla, then again, was a visionary scholar who frequently dug into the hypothetical and calculated parts of power and attraction. His initial analyses with AC power transmission, the enlistment engine, and the Tesla curl mirrored his creative and ground breaking approach. Tesla's thoughts frequently pushed the limits of traditional comprehension and prepared for extraordinary mechanical progressions.

1.3 The establishment of Edison's Menlo Park laboratory and Tesla's European education and experiences.

The late nineteenth century denoted a time of surprising development and progress in the field of electrical designing, and two of its most conspicuous figures, Thomas Edison and Nikola Tesla, were on their separate ways to significance. In this investigation, we dive into the foundation of Edison's Menlo Park research center and Tesla's European schooling and encounters. These developmental sections in their lives would shape their vocations and make a permanent imprint on the universe of science and innovation.

Edison's Menlo Park Research facility

1.1 Early Undertakings and Desires

As Thomas Edison developed as a youthful creator and business person, he held onto desires to make a lab where he could lead methodical trials and concoct new gadgets. His initial work in telecommunication and developments like the stock ticker had gathered him a few acknowledgment and monetary achievement, giving the assets expected to satisfy this fantasy.

1.2 The Area Decision: Menlo Park

In 1876, Edison procured a property in Menlo Park, New Jersey, and changed it into his incredibly famous lab complex. The decision of Menlo Park was key, as it was situated inside vicinity to significant urban communities like New York and Philadelphia. This empowered Edison to team up with different creators and access assets and markets basic to his work.

1.3 Menlo Park: The Development Manufacturing plant

Edison's lab complex in Menlo Park became known as the "creation manufacturing plant." It comprised of different structures, each committed to explicit areas of trial and error. This arrangement permitted Edison to chip away at various undertakings all the while, cultivating a climate of constant advancement.

Edison's Spearheading Work at Menlo Park

2.1 The Phonograph: Catching Sound

One of the most renowned developments to rise out of Edison's Menlo Park research center was the phonograph. In 1877, Edison and his group fostered the primary useful phonograph, a gadget fit for recording and imitating sound. This creation upset the universe of sound amusement and set up for the cutting edge music industry.

2.2 The Electric Light: Enlightening the World

Edison's mission to foster a reasonable glowing light was one of the characterizing difficulties of his profession. After endless tests and emphasess, he prevailed with regards to making a glowing light with a carbonized bamboo fiber. In 1879, Edison openly showed this progressive creation, enlightening the world with another wellspring of fake light.

2.3 The Electric Power Framework: Jolting Urban areas

Edison's work at Menlo Park reached out past individual developments; he tried to make a whole electric power framework. In 1882, he sent off the world's most memorable business electric power station on Pearl Road in New York City. This noticeable the start of metropolitan charge, with power being conveyed to homes, organizations, and roads, changing the manner in which individuals resided and worked.

Tesla's European Training and Encounters

3.1 Early Instruction and Impacts

Nikola Tesla's excursion to becoming perhaps of the most visionary designer in history started in Europe. Brought into the world in the Austrian Realm (cutting edge Croatia), Tesla got early schooling in science and physical science at the Specialized College of Graz. His encounters and impacts during this period set up for his future undertakings.

3.2 Designing Examinations in Prague and Budapest

Tesla proceeded with his schooling in designing at the Specialized College of Prague and later the Specialized College of Budapest. He succeeded in his examinations, showing a profound comprehension of electrical and mechanical designing standards. His scholarly interests furnished him with the information and abilities that would demonstrate priceless in his future trials and creations.

3.3 The Flash of Advancement: The Dynamo-Electric Machine

While concentrating on in Budapest, Tesla experienced a test that would light his energy for electrical designing. He noticed a teacher's exhibition of a Gram machine, a sort of dynamo-electric machine, and perceived shortcomings in its plan. This started Tesla's

longing to work on electrical machines, showing him a way of development that would prompt the improvement of the air conditioner enlistment engine.

The Intersection of Edison and Tesla

4.1 Tesla's Excursion to America

Nikola Tesla's profound interest with power and desire to reform electrical power frameworks in the end drove him to the US. In 1884, Tesla showed up in New York City, conveying minimal more than his thoughts and a letter of suggestion addressed to Thomas Edison. Tesla had known about Edison's accomplishments and expected to team up with the prestigious designer.

4.2 Gathering Edison and the "Battle of Flows"

Tesla's gathering with Edison denoted a urgent crossroads throughout the entire existence of power. While Tesla had expected a productive coordinated effort, their ways to deal with electrical designing separated fundamentally. Edison advocated direct flow (DC) frameworks for electrical power appropriation, while Tesla had confidence in the prevalence of exchanging flow (AC) frameworks.

This key conflict prompted what might later be known as the "Battle of Flows," an unpleasant competition between Edison's DC and Tesla's AC frameworks. Edison, distrustful of AC's security and productivity, tried to ruin it through a progression of public showings.

Edison and Tesla's Unique Ways

5.1 Edison's Proceeded with Work and Heritage

Regardless of the caustic competition with Tesla, Edison kept on making huge commitments to electrical designing and innovation. His emphasis on useful creations and advancements reached out to fields like films, telecommunication, and the improvement of the soluble stockpiling battery. Edison's inheritance as a productive designer and business visionary kept on forming the world.

5.2 Tesla's Victory with AC Power

While the "Battle of Flows" seethed on, Tesla's vision of AC power eventually won. His advancement of the air conditioner enlistment engine and transformer altered electrical power age, transmission, and conveyance. Tesla's commitments established the groundwork for the advanced electric power industry and keep on affecting electrical designing right up 'til now.

Chapter 2

Edison's Direct Current Empire

The late nineteenth century was a period of quick mechanical progression, and the field of electrical designing was at the front of development. At the core of this groundbreaking time was Thomas Edison, whose spearheading work in electrical power dispersion, especially as immediate flow (DC) frameworks, established the groundwork for the charge of urban areas and the advanced world as far as we might be concerned. In this broad investigation, we will dig into Edison's immediate flow realm, looking at the improvement of DC power frameworks, their effect on society, and the getting through tradition of Edison's commitments to electrical designing.

The Introduction of Edison's Electrical Vision

1.1 Early Tests and Business venture

Thomas Edison's interest with power started in his childhood years. His initial tests and enterprising endeavors, including offering papers and candy to prepare travelers, gave him important experiences into electrical gadgets and apparatus. Edison's initial encounters developed an enthusiasm for advancement and trial and error.

1.2 The Message and Communication

Edison's profession as a message administrator and designer during the 1860s presented him to the commonsense utilizations of power in correspondence. His advancements in telecommunication, like the stock ticker, acquired him acknowledgment and monetary dependability. This period denoted the start of Edison's excursion into the universe of electrical innovation.

Edison's Spearheading Work in Electric Lighting

2.1 The Radiant Light

Edison's most notable innovation was the radiant light, a gadget that would change indoor lighting and expand the typical business day into the evening. The improvement of the functional radiant light was a fantastic accomplishment, and Edison's orderly way to deal with trial and error assumed a critical part in its creation.

2.2 The Menlo Park Research facility

Edison laid out his Menlo Park research facility complex in New Jersey in 1876. Frequently alluded to as the "development production line," this office turned into the focal point of advancement during the late nineteenth hundred years. Edison and his group worked resolutely on a great many tasks, with an essential spotlight on consummating the glowing light.

The DC Power Framework

3.1 The Vision of Electrical Power

Edison's vision reached out past the improvement of electric lighting; he planned to make a whole electrical power framework. His objective was to give a pragmatic and safe technique for conveying power to homes and organizations. Edison trusted that immediate current (DC) was the best answer for this reason.

3.2 Pearl Road Station: The Introduction of the Principal Focal Power Plant

In 1882, Edison's vision turned into a reality with the launch of the Pearl Road Station in New York City. This noteworthy power plant, controlled by DC generators, denoted the introduction of the principal focal electrical power framework. The Pearl Road Station started the charge of urban communities, changing metropolitan scenes and businesses.

Edison's Immediate Current Realm

4.1 The Development of the DC Organization

The progress of the Pearl Road Station prompted the quick development of Edison's DC power organization. Urban areas across the US embraced the commitment of electric lighting, and power stations utilizing DC frameworks multiplied. Edison's domain of DC power was on the ascent.

4.2 Useful Applications: Road Lighting and Electric Engines

Edison's DC framework tracked down useful applications past lighting. Road lighting, once overwhelmed by gas lights, changed to electric brightening, expanding wellbeing and perceivability in metropolitan regions. Moreover, the DC framework controlled various electric engines utilized in processing plants, lifts, and trolleys, reforming ventures and transportation.

Difficulties and Impediments of DC

5.1 Voltage Drop and Restricted Reach

While Edison's DC framework was progressive, it had constraints. The transmission of power over significant distances utilizing DC presented huge difficulties because of voltage drop, which brought about energy misfortune. This impediment limited the span of DC power frameworks.

5.2 Rivalry from Substituting Current (AC)

Edison's savage contest with defenders of rotating current (AC), especially Nikola Tesla and George Westinghouse, strengthened during the "Battle of Flows." AC frameworks, with their capacity to send control over significant distances, represented an imposing danger to Edison's DC realm proficiently.

Edison's Heritage in Electrical Designing

6.1 Development and Common sense

Thomas Edison's heritage in electrical designing is portrayed by his creative soul and accentuation on common sense. He held north of

1,000 licenses, covering a great many developments, from the phonograph to the movie camera. Edison's orderly way to deal with trial and error and critical thinking made a permanent imprint on the field.

6.2 The Effect on Urbanization and Industrialization

Edison's DC power framework assumed an essential part in urbanization and industrialization. The jolt of urban communities powered financial development and worked on the personal satisfaction for a great many individuals. Businesses turned out to be more proficient and useful, driving monetary success.

The Change to Exchanging Current (AC)

7.1 The Victory of A

Regardless of Edison's assurance, the viable benefits of AC power transmission couldn't be disregarded. Nikola Tesla's advancement of the air conditioner enlistment engine and George Westinghouse's supporting of AC frameworks ended up being definitive. AC power frameworks turned into the norm for significant distance transmission and circulation.

7.2 Inheritance and Praises

As the "Battle of Flows" closed, Edison's DC realm melted away, yet his commitments to science and designing persevered. Edison got various distinctions and grants during his lifetime, including the Legislative Gold Decoration. His name became inseparable from advancement and creativity.

2.1 Edison's development of direct current (DC) electrical systems.

The late nineteenth century denoted a groundbreaking period throughout the entire existence of electrical designing, and at the very front of this upset stood Thomas Edison, a visionary creator whose work in growing direct flow (DC) electrical frameworks established the groundwork for current charge. Edison's inventive commitments and constant quest for useful arrangements changed the manner in which society produced, dispersed, and used power. In this investigation, we will dig into Edison's process in making DC electrical frameworks, investigating the key developments, challenges confronted, and the significant effect of his work.

The Early Years and Enterprising Soul

1.1. The Interest of Youthful Edison

Brought into the world on February 11, 1847, in Milan, Ohio, Thomas Edison showed an unquenchable interest since the beginning. His mom, Nancy Edison, perceived his curious nature and empowered his adoration for learning. Edison's experience growing up established the groundwork for his future as a designer and business person.

1.2. From Telecommunication to Innovation

Edison's excursion into the universe of electrical designing started during his high school years when he filled in as a message administrator. This experience presented him to the viable uses of electrical innovation, starting his interest with power and correspondence. Edison's initial profession in telecommunication gave significant experiences into electrical frameworks.

The Introduction of Edison's Imaginative Standing

2.1. Business venture Takes Off

Edison's pioneering soul arose right off the bat in his life. He participated in different undertakings, including selling papers, sweets, and vegetables to prepare travelers. These undertakings imparted in him a healthy identity dependence and monetary freedom, characteristics that would demonstrate essential in subsidizing his later tests and creations.

2.2. The Phonograph: A Milestone Innovation

In 1877, Edison revealed the phonograph, quite possibly of his most noteworthy creation. This gadget, equipped for recording and imitating sound, shocked the world and laid out Edison as an eminent creator. The phonograph exhibited his creative ability and laid the preparation for additional investigation in electrical designing.

The Foundation of Menlo Park Research center

3.1. The Introduction of the "Creation Plant"

In 1876, Edison laid out the Menlo Park lab complex in New Jersey, frequently alluded to as the "development plant." This office filled in as the focal point of Edison's imaginative undertakings, furnishing him with the assets, gear, and a talented group expected to seek after a great many ventures. Menlo Park turned into a center of development, where Edison's thoughts could come to fruition.

3.2. A Methodical Way to deal with Creation

Edison's way to deal with development was described by calculated trial and error and thorough documentation. He kept up with fastidious records of his work, recording point by point notes, portrays, and results. This methodical methodology would demonstrate important in creating down to earth electrical frameworks and developments.

Edison's Vision for Electric Lighting

4.1. The Test of Electric Lighting

Vital to Edison's work was the improvement of down to earth electric lighting. While electric curve lighting existed, it was unsatisfactory for general brightening because of its power and failure. Edison perceived the requirement for a protected, dependable, and monetarily feasible electric lighting framework that could supplant gas lighting.

4.2. The Glowing Light: An Unrest in Lighting

One of Edison's most huge forward leaps was the innovation of the brilliant light with a carbon fiber. Through broad trial and error with different materials, he found that a carbonized bamboo fiber could discharge splendid light when exposed to an electric flow. This development denoted an essential crossroads throughout the entire existence of lighting and zap.

The Introduction of Edison's Immediate Current (DC) Framework

5.1. The Common sense of DC

Edison immovably trusted that immediate flow (DC) was the best answer for conveying power to homes and organizations. DC frameworks were deeply grounded, and Edison saw their true capacity for reasonable application. His vision was to make a complete electrical power circulation framework in light of DC.

5.2. The Pearl Road Station

In 1882, Edison's vision turned into a reality with the kickoff of the Pearl Road Station in New York City. This noteworthy occasion denoted the introduction of the principal focal

electrical power station, controlled by DC generators. The Pearl Road Station denoted the start of the zap of urban areas, changing metropolitan scenes and enterprises.

Edison's DC Electrical Frameworks in real life

6.1. Development of the DC Organization

The progress of the Pearl Road Station prompted the fast development of Edison's DC power organization. Urban areas across the US embraced the commitment of electric lighting, and power stations utilizing DC frameworks multiplied. Edison's DC domain extended, enlightening roads, homes, and organizations.

6.2. Road Lighting and Electric Engines

Edison's DC framework tracked down useful applications past lighting. Road lighting, recently overwhelmed by gas lights, progressed to electric enlightenment, further developing wellbeing and perceivability in metropolitan regions. Furthermore, the DC framework fueled different electric engines utilized in plants, lifts, and trolleys, upsetting businesses and transportation.

Difficulties and Restrictions of DC

7.1. Voltage Drop and Restricted Reach

While Edison's DC framework was pivotal, it had its impediments. Communicating power over significant distances utilizing DC presented critical difficulties because of voltage drop, bringing about energy misfortune. This constraint limited the span of DC power frameworks.

7.2. Contest from Rotating Current (AC)

Edison confronted furious contest from defenders of exchanging current (AC), especially Nikola Tesla and George Westinghouse, during the "Battle of Flows." AC frameworks, with their capacity to send control over significant distances, represented an imposing test to Edison's DC realm productively.

Edison's Getting through Heritage

8.1. Development and Business venture

Thomas Edison's heritage in electrical designing is set apart by his creative soul and pioneering drive. His effect reached out past electrical frameworks to remember developments for broadcast communications, movies, from there, the sky is the limit. Edison's deliberate way to deal with trial and error and critical thinking keeps on moving ages of designers and specialists.

8.2. The Jolt of Urban communities and Businesses

Edison's DC electrical frameworks assumed a critical part in urbanization and industrialization. The jolt of urban areas energized monetary development and worked on the personal satisfaction for a huge number of individuals. Ventures turned out to be more proficient and useful, driving monetary success.

2.2 The commercialization of DC for lighting and power distribution.

The late nineteenth century was a time of fast mechanical headway, and at the front of this change was the commercialization of direct current (DC) for lighting and power dispersion. Thomas Edison, with his imaginative vision and pragmatic methodology, assumed a significant part in making DC frameworks economically reasonable. In this investigation, we will dig into the commercialization of DC for lighting and power conveyance, looking at the key achievements, challenges confronted, and the effect of this energizing turn of events.

The Introduction of Business Electric Lighting

1.1 The Gaslight Time

Before the approach of electric lighting, urban areas were transcendently enlightened by gas lights. While gas lighting was an improvement over before techniques, for example, candles and oil lights, it had constraints. Gas lighting was exorbitant, required manual activity, and presented security dangers.

1.2 Edison's Electric Light

Thomas Edison perceived the requirement for a pragmatic electric lighting arrangement. His assurance to foster a proficient and solid radiant light prompted the formation of the Edison Electric Light Organization in 1878. Edison and his group left on an excursion to market electric lighting.

The Pearl Road Station: Birth of Business Electric Power

2.1. A Focal Power Station

Edison's vision reached out past electric lighting. He expected to make a whole electrical power framework. In 1882, the Pearl Road Station in New York City turned into the world's most memorable focal electrical power station. This obvious the business birth of electric power circulation, with DC generators at the core of the framework.

2.2. DC Power Age

The Pearl Road Station utilized DC generators, principally dynamos, to create power. These machines changed mechanical energy into electrical power, providing DC flow

for lighting and different applications. The station's prosperity showed the practicality of incorporated electric power age.

The Development of the DC Organization

3.1. Metropolitan Jolt

The Pearl Road Station's prosperity incited quick metropolitan jolt. Urban communities across the US embraced electric lighting and started to take on DC power frameworks. The commitment of solid, cleaner, and more secure lighting pulled in organizations and customers the same.

3.2. Power Stations and Appropriation Organizations

The multiplication of DC power stations and dissemination networks denoted a time of extension. Edison's DC domain developed, enlightening roads, organizations, and homes. Power stations jumped up in significant urban areas, empowering power to contact more individuals and ventures.

Difficulties and Impediments

4.1. The Issue of Voltage Drop

One critical test looked by DC frameworks was voltage drop. Over significant distances, the electrical voltage would reduce, bringing about energy misfortune and diminished productivity. This limit confined the scope of DC power circulation and required the development of various little power stations.

4.2. The Conflict of Flows

Edison's DC framework confronted furious rivalry from advocates of rotating current (AC), especially Nikola Tesla and George Westinghouse. AC frameworks enjoyed a benefit in significant distance transmission because of their capacity to change voltage levels with transformers. The competition among DC and AC frameworks became known as the "Battle of Flows."

Edison's Enduring Effect

5.1. Development and Business venture

Thomas Edison's commitments reached out past electrical frameworks. His imaginative soul and enterprising mentality made a permanent imprint on the universe of innovation. Edison held north of 1,000 licenses, covering many developments, including the phonograph and films. His orderly way to deal with trial and error and critical thinking keeps on rousing designers and architects.

5.2. The Tradition of Jolt

Edison's endeavors in commercializing DC for lighting and power dissemination were instrumental in the zap of urban areas and businesses. His vision changed the manner in which individuals lived and worked, driving monetary development and working on the personal satisfaction. Edison's inheritance perseveres, with his name always connected to the charge of the advanced world.

The Change to Rotating Current (AC)

6.1. The Victory of AC

In spite of Edison's assurance, the useful benefits of rotating current (AC) transmission couldn't be ignored. Nikola Tesla's advancement of the air conditioner enlistment engine and George Westinghouse's help of AC frameworks demonstrated unequivocal. AC power transmission turned into the norm for significant distance conveyance and superseded DC in numerous applications.

6.2. Heritage and Praises

As the "Battle of Flows" finished up, Edison's DC domain steadily melted away. By the by, his commitments to science and designing were broadly perceived. Edison got various distinctions and grants during his lifetime, including the Legislative Gold Decoration. His name became inseparable from advancement and inventiveness.

2.3 Edison's rise to prominence and the founding of the Edison Electric Light Company.

The late nineteenth century denoted a groundbreaking period ever, determined by developments in innovation and power. At the core of this change stood Thomas Edison, a notable innovator and business visionary whose determined quest for down to earth arrangements prompted the jolt of urban areas and the foundation of the Edison Electric Light Organization. In this investigation, we will dig into Edison's noteworthy excursion, from his initial a very long time to his ascent to conspicuousness, and the establishing of the Edison Electric Light Organization, an essential crossroads throughout the entire existence of electrical designing.

The Early Long stretches of Thomas Edison

1.1. Youth and Instruction

Thomas Alva Edison was brought into the world on February 11, 1847, in Milan, Ohio. His childhood assumed a critical part in forming his personality and yearnings. His mom, Nancy Edison, was an instructor, and she empowered youthful Edison's affection for learning. In spite of getting a couple of long periods of formal training, Edison was an eager peruser and a self-teacher.

1.2. Innovative Endeavors

Edison's initial years were set apart by major areas of strength for an of interest and business venture. As a teen, he left on different undertakings, including selling papers, treats, and vegetables to prepare travelers. These early encounters imparted in him confidence, creativity, and a distinct fascination with reasonable uses of innovation.

The Progress to Creation

2.1. Telecommunication and Early Profession

Edison's profession in creation started when he functioned as a message administrator, first in Michigan and later in Boston. This job presented him to the prospering universe of electrical correspondence and gave bits of knowledge into the operations of transmit frameworks. Edison's work as a telegrapher established the groundwork for his future work in electrical designing.

2.2. The Time of Development

By the mid-1860s, Edison had moved to New York City, where he started chipping away at different innovations, including worked on stock tickers and vote-recording machines. These early developments denoted the start of Edison's progress from a message administrator to an undeniable innovator.

The Arrangement of Edison's Standing

3.1. The Transmitted Dash for unheard of wealth

Edison's initial developments earned respect in the message business. He got his most memorable patent for an electric vote recorder in 1869. During this period, he was granted a few licenses for developments connected with telecommunication and electrical gadgets, setting up a good foundation for himself as a creative power in the field.

3.2. The Phonograph: A Milestone Development

In 1877, Edison uncovered the phonograph, a pivotal creation that could record and replicate sound. The's first experience with the world denoted a critical second in Edison's vocation and moved him to more prominent unmistakable quality. This striking gadget exhibited his inventive capacities and caught the public's creative mind.

The Development of the Edison Electric Light Organization

4.1. The Test of Viable Electric Lighting

At the core of Edison's work was the quest for viable electric lighting. In the last part of the 1870s, gas lighting was the transcendent strategy for enlightening urban areas, yet

it had limits, including significant expense and security concerns. Edison saw a chance to alter lighting through power.

4.2. Collecting a Group

To handle the test of electric lighting, Edison collected a group of talented designers and creators. Among his key teammates were Francis Upton, Charles Batchelor, and William J. Hammer. This group would assume a critical part in fostering the innovation important for electric lighting.

Edison's Vision for Electric Lighting

5.1. A Methodical Methodology

Edison moved toward the improvement of electric lighting with a deliberate and calculated outlook. He led broad tests with different materials to track down a reasonable fiber for brilliant lights. Edison's thorough trial and error and meticulousness were signs of his way to deal with innovation.

5.2. The Radiant Light: A Distinct advantage

In 1879, Edison made a forward leap with the development of a functional brilliant light. The light included a carbon fiber that could shine splendidly when an electric flow went through it. This development denoted a defining moment in the journey for electric lighting and set up for the commercialization of Edison's vision.

Establishing the Edison Electric Light Organization

6.1. The Requirement for Commercialization

While Edison had effectively fostered a viable glowing light, the way to commercialization was laden with difficulties. To carry electric lighting to the majority, he wanted significant monetary sponsorship and a devoted association.

6.2. The Arrangement of the Organization

In 1878, Edison and his partners laid out the Edison Electric Light Organization. This organization was instrumental in getting the monetary assets expected for the enormous scope creation and conveyance of electric lighting frameworks. The organization's development denoted a vital crossroads throughout the entire existence of electrical designing.

The Pearl Road Station and the Commercialization of Power

7.1. The Pearl Road Station

In 1882, the Edison Electric Light Organization accomplished a noteworthy achievement with the launch of the Pearl Road Station in New York City. This focal power station, fueled by Edison's DC generators, turned into the world's most memorable business electric power station. It denoted the introduction of the electric utility industry and the far and wide charge of metropolitan regions.

7.2. Business Achievement and Extension

The Pearl Road Station's prosperity catalyzed the quick development of electric lighting and power circulation in metropolitan habitats. Edison's vision of pragmatic electric lighting was acknowledged as urban areas embraced electric brightening. The Edison Electric Light Organization's business achievement denoted a defining moment throughout the entire existence of electrical power.

Chapter 3

Tesla's Alternating Current Revolution

The late nineteenth century saw a significant change in the manner power was produced, sent, and used. At the core of this upheaval was Nikola Tesla, a visionary designer and specialist whose spearheading work in the field of substituting flow (AC) power redirected mechanical history as well as assumed a crucial part in forming the cutting edge world. In this 3000-word investigation, we will dig into Tesla's life, his noteworthy commitments to AC power frameworks, and the getting through tradition of his exchanging current upheaval.

1. **Tesla: A Short History**

    Prior to diving into his commitments to the field of substituting current, understanding the life and seasons of Nikola Tesla is fundamental. Brought into the world on July 10, 1856, in the town of Smiljan, in what is currently cutting edge Croatia, Tesla gave early indications of brightness and an interest with power. His process drove him from Europe to the US, where he would ultimately leave behind a legacy.

    Early Life and Schooling

    Tesla's initial schooling in designing and physical science furnished him with a solid starting point for his future work. In the wake of going to the Specialized College of Graz and the College of Prague, he left on a lifelong in electrical designing.

Appearance in the US

In 1884, Tesla showed up in the US with minimal more than whatever he might be wearing and a letter of suggestion for Thomas Edison, the noticeable creator. This experience denoted the start of a huge part in Tesla's life and the historical backdrop of power.

2. **The Conflict of Flows: Edison versus Tesla**

The late nineteenth century was a period of extraordinary contest and development in the electrical business. Two goliaths arose in this period, each upholding for an alternate technique for conveying power: Thomas Edison, a defender of direct current (DC), and Nikola Tesla, the hero of exchanging current (AC). This contention, known as the "Battle of Flows," would characterize the direction of electrical power dissemination.

The Edison Approach: Direct Current

Thomas Edison's immediate flow framework was the prevailing strategy for power circulation during the mid 1880s. DC power is portrayed by a consistent progression of electrons in a single bearing, reasonable for short-range applications yet profoundly wasteful for significant distance transmission.

Tesla's Vision: Exchanging Current

Tesla perceived the limits of DC power and supported the prevalence of exchanging current. AC power substitutes course occasionally, which makes it exceptionally appropriate for significant distance transmission and voltage change. Tesla's improvement of the air conditioner engine and transformer assumed a critical part in the possible triumph of AC over DC.

3. **Tesla's Vital Commitments to AC Power Frameworks**

Tesla's rotating flow transformation was set apart by a few critical developments and advancements that changed how power was created, sent, and used. These commitments had sweeping ramifications for the advanced world.

The Air conditioner Engine

Tesla's most renowned innovation, the rotating flow enlistment engine, reformed ventures by giving a more effective and flexible strategy for outfitting electrical power. Dissimilar to the DC engine, the air conditioner engine disposed of the requirement for a commutator, brushes, and direct electrical associations with the rotor. This advancement had significant ramifications for modern mechanization and the jolt of industrial facilities.

The Transformer

One more basic advancement by Tesla was the air conditioner transformer. This gadget considered effective voltage change, empowering the transmission of power over significant distances with insignificant misfortunes. The transformer's capacity to move forward or step down voltage levels made it a fundamental part of AC power frameworks.

The Polyphase Framework

Tesla's idea of polyphase AC power frameworks, which included the utilization of numerous stages (ordinarily three), enormously worked on the proficiency of electrical transmission. This framework considered the age and conveyance of power such that limited misfortunes and guaranteed a steady influence supply.

Tesla Curl

While the Tesla curl is frequently connected with high-voltage showings and tests, it likewise had viable applications in radio transmission and early remote correspondence. Tesla's work on thunderous circuits and the Tesla curl established the groundwork for future improvements in media communications and broadcasting.

Exchanging Current Power Lattice

Maybe Tesla's most getting through commitment was his vision of a bound together AC power network that could disperse power productively across immense distances. This idea laid the foundation for the cutting edge electrical matrix, which powers homes, organizations, and ventures around the world.

4. **The Victory of AC: Niagara Falls and Then some**

   One of the most famous showings of the prevalence of AC power was the zap of Niagara Falls. In the late nineteenth 100 years, engineers were confronted with the fantastic errand of bridling the enormous force of Niagara Tumbles to produce power for the developing interest in the US and Canada.

   The Force of Niagara Falls

   Saddling the force of Niagara Falls required a framework equipped for communicating power over significant distances to populace focuses like Bison and New York City. Tesla's AC framework, with its capacity to move forward voltage for transmission and step it down for dissemination, was the ideal arrangement.

   The Niagara Falls Power Plant

   The Niagara Falls Power Plant, planned by engineers including Tesla, George Westinghouse, and others, turned into a demonstration of the suitability of AC power transmission. At the point when it started activity in 1895, it showed that power produced at the falls could be communicated more than 20 miles to Bison, fueling businesses and illuminating the city.

   The Worldwide Spread of AC Power

   The outcome of the Niagara Falls project hardened AC as the prevailing electrical power dispersion framework. It was before long embraced in Europe, prompting the broad reception of AC power frameworks across the globe. Tesla's developments and the air conditioner power framework were instrumental in making power open to millions and driving mechanical advancement.

5. **Tesla's Vision for What's in store**

   Nikola Tesla's commitments to exchanging flow power frameworks established the groundwork for the cutting edge electrical age. Notwithstanding, his vision stretched out past the developments of his time. Tesla had excellent thoughts and developments that, however not completely acknowledged in the course of his life, keep on motivating logical and mechanical headways today.

Remote Transmission of Force

One of Tesla's most aggressive thoughts was the remote transmission of force. He accepted that power could be communicated through the air without the requirement for wires, altering how energy was dispersed. While Tesla gained some headway around here, full-scale execution of remote power transmission stays a test yet to be prevailed.

The Wardenclyffe Pinnacle

Tesla's Wardenclyffe Pinnacle, worked in Shoreham, New York, was expected to be a model for remote power transmission. Sadly, because of monetary troubles and different variables, the pinnacle was rarely finished. By and by, Tesla's vision of remote energy transmission prepared for future remote advancements, including radio and in the end, remote power move.

A Visionary Somewhat revolutionary

Tesla's cutting edge thoughts, for example, the improvement of spotless and reasonable energy sources and the idea of an overall remote correspondence framework, foreshadowed the bearing of logical and mechanical advancement in the twentieth and 21st hundreds of years. While a portion of his thoughts might have appeared to be fantastical during his lifetime, a large number of them have since become reality or are effectively being investigated.

6. Heritage and Effect

The exchanging current insurgency drove by Nikola Tesla lastingly affected the world. Tesla's commitments to electrical designing, joined with the business astuteness of George Westinghouse, prompted the far reaching reception of AC power frameworks and the foundation of the advanced electrical lattice. This heritage keeps on significantly shaping our lives in various ways.

Jolt of the World

Tesla's work on AC power frameworks assumed a crucial part in the zap of the world. The accessibility of reasonable and effective power changed ventures, worked on the personal satisfaction, and prepared for incalculable mechanical developments.

AC Power Network

The advancement of the air conditioner power framework, with its capacity to effectively communicate power over significant distances, keeps on being the foundation of present day culture. It powers homes, organizations, emergency clinics, and basic framework, making it a crucial piece of our regular routines.

Present day Innovation

The standards of AC power and the developments of Tesla are implanted in the innovation we use today. Everything from home devices to electronic gadgets depends on AC power, and the electrical lattice guarantees a steady and solid stockpile.

Logical Motivation

Tesla's work keeps on moving researchers, architects, and innovators around the world. His creative soul and commitment to pushing the limits of innovation act as a model for those looking to make forward leaps in science and designing.

3.1 Nikola Tesla's groundbreaking work on alternating current (AC).

Nikola Tesla, a visionary designer and electrical specialist brought into the world in 1856, is maybe most popular for his notable work on substituting flow (AC) power. Tesla's commitments to AC power frameworks upset how power is produced, communicated, and used, eventually molding the cutting edge world. In this investigation, we'll dig into the vital parts of Tesla's work on AC and the significant effect it has had on our lives.

1. **Prologue to Exchanging Current**

   Direct Flow (DC): In a DC framework, electric charge streams consistently in one bearing, from the positive terminal to the adverse terminal. Thomas Edison, a contemporary of Tesla, supported DC as the essential strategy for electrical power conveyance.

   Substituting Flow (AC): AC, then again, is portrayed by an occasional inversion of the heading of electric charge stream. The ongoing switches back and forth among positive and negative stages, which permits it to quickly take an alternate route. Tesla was an intense backer of AC as a more proficient and flexible technique for power conveyance.

2. **Tesla's Initial Work and Training**

   Nikola Tesla's interest with power was obvious since early on. In the wake of finishing his schooling in designing and physical science at foundations like the Specialized College of Graz and the College of Prague, Tesla left on a vocation that would prompt various leap forwards in electrical designing.

   Tesla's Apprenticeship and Early Work

   Tesla started his profession by working for broadcast organizations in Europe, where he acquired commonsense involvement with electrical designing. He later moved to the US, where he looked for work with, in all honesty, Thomas Edison himself.

   Appearance in the US

   In 1884, Tesla showed up in the US fully intent on working close by Edison, the noticeable designer of the time. Be that as it may, their varying perspectives on electrical frameworks and the popular "Battle of Flows" would before long put them in conflict.

3. **The Conflict of Flows: Tesla versus Edison**

   The late nineteenth century saw a wild fight between defenders of DC and AC frameworks, frequently alluded to as the "Battle of Flows." Tesla and Edison were the focal figures in this contention, upholding for their separate advancements.

Edison's DC Framework

Thomas Edison's immediate flow (DC) framework was the prevailing technique for electrical power dissemination during the mid 1880s. It included the utilization of DC generators and expected power stations at generally short spans because of critical power misfortune over distance.

Tesla's Vision: Exchanging Current

Tesla, then again, put stock in the predominance of exchanging current (AC) for significant distance transmission. AC's capacity to quickly switch the course of electric charge stream made it more proficient for high-voltage transmission and less inclined to drive misfortune over significant distances.

Tesla's Forward leap: The Air conditioner Engine

One of Tesla's most critical commitments to AC power frameworks was the innovation of the rotating current enlistment engine. Not at all like DC engines, AC engines wiped out the requirement for a commutator and brushes, which made them more productive, solid, and flexible. This development denoted a defining moment in the "Battle of Flows."

4. **Key Commitments to AC Power Frameworks**

   Tesla's spearheading work on AC power frameworks went past the creation of the air conditioner engine. His commitments to the field were various and had expansive ramifications for the world.

The Transformer

Tesla's improvement of the air conditioner transformer was another basic headway. Transformers considered productive voltage change, making it conceivable to send power over significant distances with insignificant misfortunes. The capacity to move forward or step down voltage levels was fundamental for the progress of AC power circulation.

The Polyphase Framework

Tesla's idea of polyphase AC power frameworks, normally

utilizing three stages, fundamentally worked on the proficiency of electrical transmission. This approach considered the age and dissemination of power in a way that limited misfortunes and guaranteed a steady influence supply.

Exchanging Current Power Network

Maybe Tesla's most persevering through commitment was his vision of a bound together AC power lattice that could disperse power effectively across tremendous distances. This idea established the groundwork for the advanced electrical framework, which powers homes, organizations, and enterprises around the world.

5. **The Victory of AC: The Zap of Niagara Falls**

One of the most famous exhibitions of the predominance of AC power was the zap of Niagara Falls, a venture that displayed the capacity of AC frameworks for huge scope power age and significant distance transmission.

Tackling the Force of Niagara Falls

Niagara Falls, with its gigantic water stream, offered a colossal chance for producing power. Engineers confronted the test of sending this control over significant distances to satisfy the energy needs of neighboring urban areas.

The Niagara Falls Power Plant

Tesla, in a joint effort with George Westinghouse and different specialists, assumed a key part in planning the Niagara Falls Power Plant. At the point when it started activity in 1895, the plant showed that power produced at the falls could be communicated north of 20 miles to Bison, New York, actually fueling ventures and illuminating the city.

Worldwide Reception of AC Power

The progress of the Niagara Falls project set AC as the predominant electrical power dissemination framework. Europe immediately stuck to this same pattern, prompting the inescapable reception of AC power frameworks across the globe. Tesla's creations and the air conditioner power network were instrumental in making power open to millions and driving mechanical advancement.

6. Tesla's Heritage and Effect

Nikola Tesla's commitments to exchanging current power frameworks made history. His work, joined with the visionary business techniques of George Westinghouse, brought about the broad reception of AC as the essential strategy for electrical power appropriation.

Jolt of the World

Tesla's advancements in AC power frameworks changed ventures and worked on the personal satisfaction for individuals all over the planet. The accessibility of reasonable and effective power prepared for innovative headways and monetary development.

Present day Innovation

Tesla's standards and innovations support a significant part of the innovation we use today. From home devices to electronic gadgets, essentially every part of our regular routines depends on AC power and the electrical network that Tesla laid out.

Logical Motivation

Tesla's work keeps on rousing researchers, designers, and innovators. His devotion to pushing the limits of innovation fills in as a model for those trying to make notable progressions in science and designing.

3.2 The advantages of AC over DC in long-distance power transmission.

The fight between rotating flow (AC) and direct flow (DC) for strength in the domain of electrical power dissemination, frequently alluded to as the "Battle of Flows," was one of the main mechanical struggles of the late nineteenth 100 years. While DC had its benefits, AC at last arose as the reasonable champ, especially in significant distance power transmission. In this conversation, we will investigate the upsides of AC over DC with regards to significant distance power transmission, which established the groundwork for the advanced electrical network and changed the manner in which we outfit and disseminate electrical energy.

1. **The Verifiable Setting: The Conflict of Flows**

   Prior to digging into the particular benefits of AC in significant distance power transmission, understanding the authentic setting in which this fight unfolded is fundamental.

   Thomas Edison and DC

   Thomas Edison, an unmistakable designer and business person, was a steadfast promoter of direct current (DC) power frameworks. He accepted that DC was more secure and more controllable than AC, making it appropriate for lighting and early modern applications. Edison's DC framework, known as the Edison framework, used DC generators and required power stations at somewhat short stretches.

   Nikola Tesla and AC

   Nikola Tesla, a splendid designer and creator, supported substituting flow (AC) as a predominant strategy for electrical power circulation. He trusted that air conditioner's capacity to occasionally switch the bearing of electric charge stream made it more effective for high-voltage transmission and less inclined to control misfortune over significant distances.

2. **The Upsides of AC in Significant Distance Power Transmission**

   Voltage Change with Transformers

   One of the main benefits of AC over DC in significant distance power transmission is the capacity to effectively change the voltage level utilizing transformers. Transformers can move forward (increment) or step down (decline) voltage on a case by case basis. This element is critical for limiting power misfortunes during transmission.

   At the point when electrical energy is communicated at high voltages, the flow is diminished, bringing about lower resistive misfortunes (I^2R misfortunes) in the

transmission lines. Transformers at substations close to the well-spring of force age move forward the voltage, permitting power to be sent proficiently over significant

distances. Close to the objective, transformers step down the voltage for safe conveyance to customers.

Diminished Power Misfortunes

The peculiarity of force misfortune because of opposition in transmission lines is a huge worry in significant distance influence transmission. In DC frameworks, power misfortune is straightforwardly corresponding to the square of the current ($P = I^2R$), and that implies that communicating influence at high voltages is less effective.

Interestingly, AC frameworks can send power at high voltages while keeping current generally low. Since power misfortune is corresponding to current squared, AC transmission lines experience fundamentally less resistive misfortunes contrasted with DC lines over significant distances. This productivity in power transmission is a pivotal benefit of AC.

Simplicity of Voltage Transformation

AC power frameworks offer the adaptability to change voltage levels effectively and proficiently utilizing transformers. This adaptability is fundamental for adjusting the voltage to various prerequisites all through the electrical matrix. For example, power can be moved forward for significant distance transmission, ventured down for appropriation, and further adapted to explicit modern or private applications.

Conversely, DC frameworks miss the mark on same level of adaptability with regards to voltage transformation. Changing over DC voltage levels commonly requires perplexing and less proficient electronic transformation processes.

Straightforwardness in Age and Dispersion

AC power age is moderately clear. Most power plants, whether they utilize petroleum products, thermal power, or sustainable sources like breeze or hydropower, create AC power. This straightforwardness adjusts well to the simplicity of AC conveyance and voltage change.

Conversely, DC age can be more complicated, as it frequently requires changing over the produced AC power into DC before dissemination. This extra step acquaints failures and intricacy with the framework.

Synchronization in Networks

In interconnected power networks, guaranteeing that all generators are synchronized is vital to keeping a steady and dependable power supply. AC power intrinsically fits synchronization in light of the fact that the recurrence (commonly 60 Hz in North America and 50 Hz in numerous different districts) guarantees that all generators and burdens work in stage.

In DC frameworks, accomplishing synchronization is seriously difficult, as DC doesn't intrinsically have a recurrence part like AC. This trouble can prompt functional difficulties in keeping a decent and synchronized matrix.

Capacitive and Inductive Reactance

AC circuits show capacitive and inductive reactance, which can assist with overseeing power factor rectification. Power factor revision guarantees that the electrical power provided by utilities is proficiently utilized and limits energy squander. AC power frameworks can be intended to alleviate power factor issues, making them more versatile to assorted burdens and enterprises.

Interestingly, DC frameworks don't normally display similar capacitive and inductive qualities, making power factor adjustment really testing and less proficient.

3. **The Job of Transformers in AC Transmission**

The focal job of transformers in AC power transmission couldn't possibly be more significant. These gadgets take into consideration effective voltage change, which is urgent for limiting power misfortunes over significant distances.

Move forward Transformers

At power age stations, move forward transformers increment the voltage of the created AC power to levels reasonable for significant distance transmission. Higher voltage diminishes the ongoing moving through transmission lines, essentially diminishing resistive misfortunes.

Step-Down Transformers

Close to the objective or buyer locales, step-down transformers lessen the voltage to protected and usable levels. This change guarantees that power can be disseminated successfully for different applications, including private, business, and modern use.

Transmission Productivity

The blend of move forward and step-down transformers in AC transmission frameworks boosts transmission proficiency while keeping up with the wellbeing and convenience of power. This productivity is a huge benefit while sending control over broad lattices and across significant distances.

4. Verifiable Achievements: The Job of Tesla and Westinghouse

The effective execution of AC power transmission over significant distances was put forth conceivable by the cooperative attempts of Nikola Tesla and George

Westinghouse, who perceived the upsides of AC and worked vigorously to create and advance this framework.

Tesla's Developments

Nikola Tesla's developments, including the air conditioner engine and the air conditioner transformer, were instrumental in exhibiting the capability of AC power frameworks. His pivotal work established the groundwork for the productive transmission of electrical energy.

George Westinghouse's Business Sharpness

George Westinghouse, a business visionary and specialist, perceived the capability of Tesla's AC framework and its benefits over Edison's

DC framework. Westinghouse's organization, Westinghouse Electric, turned into a key part in the turn of events and sending of AC power frameworks, including the development of force plants and transmission lines.

The Niagara Falls Power Plant

One of the most famous shows of AC power's viability in significant distance transmission was the zap of Niagara Falls. The Niagara Falls Power Plant, planned by engineers including Tesla and Westinghouse, exhibited the capacity to send power created at the falls more than 20 miles to Bison, New York. This venture's prosperity cemented AC's situation as the favored strategy for significant distance power transmission.

3.3 The challenges and triumphs in Tesla's efforts to promote AC technology.

Nikola Tesla's persevering endeavors to advance and progress rotating flow (AC) innovation denoted an essential section throughout the entire existence of power. His work confronted various difficulties, both specialized and individual, as he tried to exhibit the prevalence of AC over direct current (DC). Regardless of these obstructions, Tesla's victories in promoting AC power frameworks established the groundwork for current electrical matrices and changed the manner in which we create, send, and use power. In this conversation, we will dive into the difficulties Tesla experienced and the momentous victories he accomplished in his main goal to advance AC innovation.

1. **The Early Difficulties: Laying out Believability and Acknowledgment**

    Contending with Thomas Edison

    One of Tesla's essential difficulties was contending with the considerable Thomas Edison, who was a deeply grounded figure in the realm of power. Edison was a backer for DC power frameworks and had a strong presence in the business. Tesla, a somewhat obscure settler from Europe, confronted the overwhelming errand of testing Edison's perspectives and earning respect for his thoughts on AC.

Acquiring Monetary Help

Tesla's visionary thoughts required significant monetary sponsorship for innovative work. At different places in his vocation, he battled to get the financing expected to direct analyses, construct models, and demonstrate the practicality of AC power frameworks

Specialized Difficulties

Tesla's work on AC innovation included beating a progression of specialized difficulties. Creating productive transformers, engines, and power dissemination frameworks was a complicated and requesting task that expected both development and determination.

2. **Wins in Advancing AC Innovation**

The Air conditioner Engine

One of Tesla's most huge victories was the development of the substituting current acceptance engine. This progressive gadget dispensed with the requirement for commutators and brushes, which were intrinsic disadvantages of DC engines. AC engines were more proficient, dependable, and flexible, settling on them a predominant decision for modern applications.

Tesla's fruitful exhibition of the air conditioner engine's capacities displayed the capability of AC innovation to outflank DC in different ventures, especially in driving apparatus and computerizing plants. His development established the groundwork for the far and wide reception of AC engines, which are as yet involved today in endless applications, from domestic devices to modern apparatus.

The Tesla Loop

Tesla's development of the Tesla loop was another surprising victory. While it had prompt applications in high-recurrence and high-voltage tries, the Tesla curl likewise caught the public's creative mind. It turned into an image of logical development and assisted Tesla with earning respect and backing for his work.

The Tesla curl's capacity to create high-voltage, high-recurrence electrical releases made it a well known fascination for public showings and presentations. Tesla utilized these exhibitions not exclusively to grandstand the capacities of AC innovation yet additionally to create interest and backing for his bigger vision of a world controlled by AC power.

Coordinated effort with George Westinghouse

Maybe one of Tesla's most huge victories was his joint effort with industrialist and business person George Westinghouse. Perceiving the capability of AC power frameworks, Westinghouse collaborated with Tesla to create and advance AC innovation.

Westinghouse Electric, under Tesla's direction, turned into a central part in the turn of events and organization of AC power frameworks. The organization tied down agreements to assemble AC power plants and transmission lines, including the notorious Niagara Falls Power Plant. This undertaking, which exhibited the plausibility of communicating power over significant distances utilizing AC, was a resonating achievement and assumed a urgent part in the reception of AC power frameworks around the world.

The Victory at the Chicago World's Fair

Tesla's endeavors to advance AC innovation got a huge lift with the effective exhibit of AC power at the 1893 Chicago World's Fair, otherwise called the World's Columbian Composition. Westinghouse Electric won the agreement to give electrical capacity to the fair, and Tesla's AC framework was placed to the test for a great scope.

The fair highlighted a stunning presentation of electrical lighting, including the brightening of the carnival and the world's most memorable electrically lit city roads. The outcome of the fair's electrical establishments, fueled by AC innovation, was a defining moment in the "Battle of Flows." It not just shown the reasonableness and security of AC power yet additionally caught the public's creative mind and prompted a flood popular for AC frameworks.

The Foundation of AC Power Networks

One of Tesla's most persevering through wins was the foundation of AC power matrices. Tesla's vision of a bound together AC power network that could productively disseminate power over huge distances turned into a reality. The Air conditioner power matrix that we depend on today to drive homes, organizations, and enterprises overall owes its presence to Tesla's spearheading work.

The progress of the Niagara Falls Power Plant and ensuing ventures hardened AC as the predominant strategy for significant distance power transmission. This shift away from DC frameworks denoted a great victory for Tesla's vision and added to the quick zap of the world.

3. **The Difficulties Inside: Individual and Monetary Battles**

While Tesla accomplished exceptional victories in advancing AC innovation, he confronted huge individual and monetary difficulties all through his vocation.

Monetary Battles

Tesla's desires frequently dominated his monetary assets. He got subsidizing for certain ventures through organizations and speculations, yet he additionally experienced times of monetary difficulty. His commitment to propelling science and innovation at times overshadowed monetary benefit.

Individual Battles

Tesla's extreme spotlight on his work in some cases came at the expense of his own life and prosperity. He was known for his unconventionalities and episodes of over the top way of behaving. Tesla's determined devotion to his work was both a strength and a test, as it once in a while prompted disregarding pragmatic parts of his own and monetary undertakings.

Contentions and Patent Fights

Tesla confronted competitions and patent fights with different innovators and organizations. His debates with figures like Thomas Edison and Guglielmo Marconi were irrefutable. These contentions, while depleting, additionally featured the seriousness of the period and the stakes engaged with the competition to create and control electrical advances.

4. The Tradition of Tesla's Victories

Nikola Tesla's victories in advancing AC innovation passed on a permanent heritage that keeps on forming our reality. His commitments to AC power frameworks, including the air conditioner engine, transformer innovation, and the advancement of the air conditioner power network, upset how power is produced, sent, and used.

The Cutting edge Electrical Network

Tesla's vision of a bound together AC power network stays the foundation of present day electrical framework. The electrical framework, controlled by AC innovation, empowers the solid and effective appropriation of power to homes, organizations, and businesses. It is the foundation of present day human progress and a demonstration of Tesla's foreknowledge.

Jolt and Development

Tesla's work on AC innovation sped up the jolt of the world, carrying electrical ability to even the most distant districts. This jolt worked on the personal satisfaction as well as powered mechanical developments and monetary development.

Logical Motivation

Tesla's victories in elevating AC innovation keep on rousing researchers, specialists, and designers. His devotion to pushing the limits of innovation fills in as a model for those trying to make momentous headways in science and designing.

Public Mindfulness and Acknowledgment

Lately, Nikola Tesla has earned restored respect and appreciation for his commitments to science and innovation. His name is inseparable from advancement and the quest for visionary thoughts. Tesla's heritage lives on in the various books, films, and social references that praise his life and work.

Chapter 4

The War of Currents

The late nineteenth century was a time of quick mechanical progression and development, especially in the field of power. At the focal point of this change was an unpleasant contention known as the "Battle of Flows," a fight between two monsters of the electrical business: Thomas Edison and Nikola Tesla. This energizing struggle fixated on the decision between two contending strategies for electrical power transmission — direct flow (DC) and rotating flow (AC). In this complete investigation, we will dive into the beginnings, vital participants, advancements, and outcomes of the Conflict of Flows, revealing insight into the significant effect it had on the universe of power and society at large.

1. **Foundation: The Ascent of Power in the Late nineteenth 100 years**

   To comprehend the Conflict of Flows, getting a handle on the verifiable setting of the late nineteenth hundred years and the quick ascent of power as a groundbreaking force is fundamental.

   Early Trailblazers of Power

   The mid-nineteenth century saw the development of trailblazers like Michael Faraday, André-Marie Ampère, and Georg Ohm, who laid the preparation for the comprehension of power and attraction. Their revelations made ready for functional uses of power.

Innovation of the Light

Thomas Edison's improvement of the down to earth glowing light in 1879 denoted a critical achievement throughout the entire existence of power. This development vowed to carry protected and solid enlightenment to homes and organizations, starting the interest for electrical power.

The Requirement for Electrical Power Dissemination

As the interest for electric lighting developed, so did the requirement for proficient techniques for disseminating electrical control over significant distances. The underlying test was to devise a framework that could communicate power from power stations to homes and organizations.

2. **The Competitors: Thomas Edison and Direct Current (DC)**

Thomas Edison, known as the "Wizard of Menlo Park," was a praised designer and business visionary who supported the utilization of direct flow (DC) for electrical power dispersion.

Edison's Immediate Current (DC) Framework

Edison's DC framework depended on generators that created a consistent progression of electric flow in one heading. This framework was successful for brief distance transmission however experienced huge power misfortune over longer distances.

The Edison Electric Light Organization

Edison laid out the Edison Electric Light Organization in 1878 to create and advertise his radiant light and the related electrical framework. He introduced DC power frameworks in different urban areas to give electric lighting.

Edison's Perspectives on AC

Edison was at first incredulous of rotating current (AC) frameworks, frequently scrutinizing them as perilous and doubtful. He was profoundly put resources into advancing his own DC framework and saw AC as a danger to his financial matters.

3. **The Challenger: Nikola Tesla and Exchanging Current (AC)**
Nikola Tesla, a splendid Serbian-American designer and electrical specialist, arose as the main defender of substituting flow (AC) innovation — a framework he accepted to be infinitely better to DC for significant distance power transmission.

Tesla's Initial Vocation

Tesla started his vocation working for the Mainland Edison Organization in Paris, where he acquired reasonable involvement in electrical frameworks. He later moved to the US, showing up in 1884.

The Polyphase AC Framework

Tesla fostered the idea of the polyphase AC framework, which included the utilization of different stages (normally three) of rotating current. This framework offered superior productivity and considered the transmission of power over significant distances with negligible power misfortune.

The Air conditioner Enlistment Engine

Tesla's most praised development was the air conditioner enlistment engine, which wiped out the requirement for a commutator and brushes, normal parts in DC engines. AC engines were more proficient, strong, and flexible, making them ideal for modern applications.

The Tesla Curl

Tesla likewise concocted the Tesla loop, a high-recurrence transformer that created high-voltage electrical releases. While at first utilized in high-recurrence explores, the Tesla loop turned into an image of logical development and caught the public's creative mind.

4. **The Heightening of the Conflict: Tesla versus Edison**
The competition among Tesla and Edison raised as they advanced their separate electrical frameworks and took part in a fight for

strength in the developing electrical industry.

Tesla's Endeavors to Advance AC

Not entirely set in stone to show the upsides of AC over DC. He got licenses for his AC engine and polyphase framework and tried to popularize his innovations. His aggressive objective was to make a bound together AC power framework that could proficiently send power over significant distances.

The Support of George Westinghouse

Tesla's vision got a critical lift when he cooperated with George Westinghouse, an effective industrialist and business person. Westinghouse perceived the capability of AC innovation and considered Tesla's creations to be a method for testing Edison's DC framework.

The Fight Over the Chicago World's Fair

The Chicago World's Fair of 1893 introduced a chance for Tesla and Westinghouse to exhibit the capacities of AC power on a stupendous scale. Westinghouse Electric won the agreement to give electrical capacity to the fair, and Tesla's AC framework was exhibited in a stunning showcase of electrical lighting.

The effective zap of the carnival and the world's most memorable electrically lit city roads exhibited the common sense and security of AC power. It was a defining moment in the Conflict of Flows and caught the public's creative mind, prompting expanded interest for AC innovation.

5. **The Victory of AC: Niagara Falls and Then some**

One of the most notorious victories of AC innovation was the charge of Niagara Falls, a task that exhibited the capacities of AC power on an extraordinary scale.

Bridling the Force of Niagara Falls

Niagara Falls introduced a novel chance for creating power for a huge scope. Engineers confronted the test of sending this control over significant distances to fulfill the energy needs of adjacent urban communities.

The Niagara Falls Power Plant

Tesla, in a joint effort with Westinghouse and different specialists, assumed a significant part in planning the Niagara Falls Power Plant. At the point when it started activity in 1895, the plant exhibited that power created at the falls could be sent more than 20 miles to Bison, New York, actually fueling enterprises and illuminating the city.

Worldwide Reception of AC Power

The outcome of the Niagara Falls project set AC as the predominant electrical power dissemination framework. It was before long embraced in Europe, prompting the far and wide acknowledgment of AC power frameworks across the globe. Tesla's creations and the air conditioner power framework were instrumental in making power open to millions and driving mechanical advancement.

6. Heritage and Effect of the Conflict of Flows

The Conflict of Flows lastingly affected the universe of power and innovation. The victory of AC innovation, supported by Nikola Tesla and George Westinghouse, established the groundwork for the advanced electrical framework and changed the manner in which we create, communicate, and use power.

The Advanced Electrical Lattice

Tesla's vision of a brought together AC power lattice turned into a reality and stays the foundation of current electrical framework. The electrical network powers homes, organizations, emergency clinics, and basic foundation, guaranteeing a dependable and productive inventory of power.

Jolt and Advancement

The inescapable reception of AC innovation sped up the zap of the world, working on the personal satisfaction and filling mechanical developments. Power turned into a main impetus behind industrialization, mechanization, and mechanical advancement in the twentieth 100 years.

Logical Motivation

Tesla's devotion to pushing the limits of innovation keeps on rousing researchers, specialists, and creators around the world. His imaginative soul and obligation to progressing electrical designing act as a model for those trying to make notable headways in science and innovation.

Public Mindfulness and Acknowledgment

Lately, Nikola Tesla has earned recharged respect and appreciation for his commitments to science and innovation. His name is inseparable from development and the quest for visionary thoughts. Tesla's heritage lives on in various books, films, and social references that commend his life and work.

4.1 The intense rivalry between Edison's DC and Tesla's AC systems.

The late nineteenth century saw a savage and sensational competition between two spearheading figures in the field of electrical designing: Thomas Edison and Nikola Tesla. This competition, known as the "Battle of Flows," rotated around the contending frameworks of electrical power transmission — direct flow (DC) and substituting flow (AC). The extreme rivalry between Edison's DC framework and Tesla's AC framework molded the course of electrical designing as well as had extensive ramifications for the charge of the world. In this investigation, we will dive into the subtleties of this memorable contention, featuring the central members, the fight for matchless quality, the specialized contrasts, and the significant effect on society.

1. **Foundation: The Ascent of Electrical Power**

    To comprehend the competition among Edison and Tesla, it's urgent to perceive the verifiable setting wherein it unfurled — a period set apart by quick progressions in electrical innovation and the developing interest for electric power.

    The Development of Electrical Trend-setters

During the nineteenth hundred years, different creators and researchers made huge commitments to the comprehension of power and attraction. Trailblazers like Michael Faraday, André-Marie Ampère, and Georg Ohm laid the foundation for viable uses of power.

Edison's Innovation of the Brilliant Light

One of the significant crossroads throughout the entire existence of power was Thomas Edison's effective improvement of the functional glowing light in 1879. This creation offered a dependable and proficient method for brightening and lighted an interest for electrical power.

The Requirement for Power Circulation

Edison's innovation of the light raised the test of fostering a framework to send electrical control over significant distances proficiently. A technique for electrical dispersion was expected to bring power into homes, organizations, and businesses.

2. ## Thomas Edison and Direct Current (DC)

Thomas Edison, frequently alluded to as the "Wizard of Menlo Park," assumed a focal part in the early jolt of the US. He advocated the utilization of direct flow (DC) for electrical power conveyance.

Edison's Immediate Current (DC) Framework

Edison's DC framework depended on generators that created a ceaseless progression of electric flow in one course, from the positive to the adverse terminal. This immediate and consistent progression of flow was viewed as safe for early electrical applications.

The Development of the Edison Electric Light Organization

In 1878, Edison laid out the Edison Electric Light Organization, determined to create and advertising his glowing light and the foundation important to give electric lighting administrations. He started introducing DC power frameworks in different urban areas to supply power to buyers.

Resistance to Rotating Current (AC)

Edison was at first incredulous of exchanging flow (AC) frameworks, which included intermittent inversions of the bearing of electric charge stream. He censured AC as perilous and dubious, frequently openly showing the alleged risks of high-voltage AC.

3. **Nikola Tesla and Exchanging Current (AC)**

Nikola Tesla, a splendid Serbian-American designer and electrical specialist, arose as the main defender of exchanging flow (AC) innovation — a framework he accepted was better than DC for significant distance power transmission.

Tesla's Initial Profession

Tesla started his profession working for the Mainland Edison Organization in Paris, acquiring useful involvement in electrical frameworks. He moved to the US in 1884 and immediately became famous in the realm of electrical designing.

The Polyphase AC Framework

Tesla fostered the idea of the polyphase AC framework, which included the utilization of various stages (commonly three) of substituting current. This framework offered better productivity and took into account the transmission of power over significant distances with negligible power misfortune.

The Air conditioner Acceptance Engine

Tesla's most commended development was the air conditioner enlistment engine, which dispensed with the requirement for a commutator and brushes — normal parts in DC engines. AC engines were more proficient, solid, and adaptable, making them ideal for modern applications.

The Tesla Loop

Tesla likewise imagined the Tesla loop, a high-recurrence transformer fit for producing high-voltage electrical releases. While at first utilized in high-recurrence tries, the Tesla loop caught the public's creative mind and turned into an image of logical development.

4. **The Acceleration of the Conflict: Edison versus Tesla**

The contention among Edison and Tesla raised as they advanced their separate electrical frameworks and participated in a fight for predominance in the developing electrical industry.

Tesla's Endeavors to Advance AC

Not set in stone to show the upsides of AC over DC. He got licenses for his AC engine and polyphase framework and looked to popularize his creations. His aggressive objective was to make a brought together AC power lattice that could productively send power over significant distances.

Sponsorship of George Westinghouse

Tesla's vision got a huge lift when he collaborated with George Westinghouse, an effective industrialist and business person. Westinghouse perceived the capability of AC innovation and considered Tesla's creations to be a method for testing Edison's DC framework.

The Fight Over the Chicago World's Fair

The Chicago World's Fair of 1893 introduced a chance for Tesla and Westinghouse to exhibit the capacities of AC power on a fabulous scale. Westinghouse Electric won the agreement to give electrical capacity to the fair, and Tesla's AC framework was exhibited in a stunning showcase of electrical lighting.

The fruitful charge of the carnival and the world's most memorable electrically lit city roads showed the reasonableness and security of AC power. It was a defining moment in the Conflict of Flows and caught the public's creative mind, prompting expanded interest for AC innovation.

5. **The Victory of AC: Niagara Falls and Then some**

One of the most famous victories of AC innovation was the jolt of Niagara Falls, a task that exhibited the capacities of AC power on a phenomenal scale.

Tackling the Force of Niagara Falls

Niagara Falls introduced a one of a kind chance for creating power for an enormous scope. Engineers confronted the test of sending this control over significant distances to fulfill the energy needs of adjacent urban areas.

The Niagara Falls Power Plant

Tesla, as a team with Westinghouse and different specialists, assumed a significant part in planning the Niagara Falls Power Plant. At the point when it started activity in 1895, the plant showed that power produced at the falls could be communicated more than 20 miles to Bison, New York, really driving businesses and illuminating the city.

Worldwide Reception of AC Power

The outcome of the Niagara Falls project set AC as the predominant electrical power circulation framework. It was before long taken on in Europe, prompting the far reaching acknowledgment of AC power frameworks across the globe. Tesla's developments and the air conditioner power network were instrumental in making power available to millions and driving mechanical advancement.

6. **The Heritage and Effect of the Conflict of Flows**

The Conflict of Flows lastingly affected the universe of power and innovation. The victory of AC innovation, advocated by Nikola Tesla and George Westinghouse, established the groundwork for the cutting edge electrical framework and changed the manner in which we produce, send, and use power.

The Cutting edge Electrical Framework

Tesla's vision of a bound together AC power framework turned into a reality and stays the foundation of current electrical framework. The electrical matrix powers homes, organizations, medical clinics, and basic framework, guaranteeing a dependable and productive stock of power.

Jolt and Development

The inescapable reception of AC innovation sped up the jolt of the world, working on the personal satisfaction and filling mechanical developments. Power turned into a main impetus behind industrialization, mechanization, and mechanical advancement in the twentieth 100 years.

Logical Motivation

Tesla's commitment to pushing the limits of innovation keeps on rousing researchers, designers, and innovators around the world. His creative soul and obligation to progressing electrical designing act as a model for those looking to make momentous headways in science and innovation.

Public Mindfulness and Acknowledgment

Lately, Nikola Tesla has earned recharged respect and appreciation for his commitments to science and innovation. His name is inseparable from advancement and the quest for visionary thoughts. Tesla's heritage lives on in various books, films, and social references that praise his life and work.

4.2 The media and public perceptions of the "War of Currents."

The "Battle of Flows," the serious competition between Thomas Edison's immediate flow (DC) and Nikola Tesla's exchanging flow (AC) frameworks for electrical power transmission in the late nineteenth 100 years, was a clash of innovation as well as a skirmish of stories. The media assumed a critical part in molding public view of this memorable struggle, which had broad ramifications for the jolt of the world. In this investigation, we will dive into how the media covered the Conflict of Flows, the public's responses and discernments, and the enduring effect of this media-driven story.

1. **The Media Scene of the Late nineteenth 100 years**

    To comprehend the media's part in forming view of the Conflict of Flows, it's fundamental to consider the media scene of the late nineteenth hundred years.

    Print Media Predominance

    Print media, including papers and magazines, were the essential wellsprings of data and news spread during this period. Papers had huge reach and impact, with various distributions taking special care of different crowds.

Restricted Media sources

Contrasted with the present large number of media sources, there were somewhat less papers and magazines available for use. Be that as it may, these distributions had significant readership and filled in as persuasive stages for molding general assessment.

Mechanical Progressions

Progressions in printing innovation, for example, the linotype machine, made paper creation more effective and considered expanded flow and conveyance.

2. **The Trailblazers: Edison and Tesla**

The media's inclusion of the Conflict of Flows generally focused on the two essential figures behind the contending electrical frameworks — Thomas Edison and Nikola Tesla.

Edison's Media Keen

Thomas Edison was a creator as well as a gifted advertising expert. He perceived the significance of media inclusion and effectively drew in with writers to advance his DC framework. Edison's superstar status and media-accommodating persona made him a conspicuous figure in reports.

Tesla's Advancements

Nikola Tesla, while a splendid designer, was less media-wise than Edison. He zeroed in more on his examination and developments than on pursuing media consideration. This distinction in approach would have suggestions for how the media depicted the two creators.

3. **Media Stories: Edison versus Tesla**

The media stories that arose during the Conflict of Flows were affected by a few elements, including the creators' characters, the contending innovations, and the business interests in question.

Edison as the Laid out Legend

Thomas Edison, currently notable for his development of the

phonograph and the brilliant light, was many times depicted as a legend and an image of American development. The media celebrated him as an independent virtuoso and a hero of safe electrical frameworks.

Tesla's Strange Persona

Nikola Tesla, paradoxically, was depicted as a more puzzling and unpredictable figure. His hesitance to draw in with the media and his flighty thoughts, like remote transmission of force, added to his depiction as a cryptic virtuoso.

The Clash of Flows

The media outlined the contention between Edison's DC and Tesla's AC frameworks as a sensational "Skirmish of Flows." This outlining added a feeling of contention and rivalry to the story, making it more captivating for perusers.

Wellbeing Concerns and Manipulation through scare tactics

To create titles and catch perusers' consideration, a few papers and magazines misrepresented the dangers related with AC frameworks. High-voltage AC exhibitions were sensationalized, prompting public apprehensions of electric shock and risk.

Media Inclusion of Public Showings

Both Edison and Tesla directed public exhibits to feature the wellbeing and viability of their individual frameworks. These shows frequently collected broad media inclusion, impacting public discernments.

4. Public Responses and Discernments

The media's inclusion of the Conflict of Flows significantly affected public discernments, prompting a blend of energy, dread, and interest.

Feeling of dread toward Power

A few news sources hyped the risks of high-voltage AC, adding to a feeling of dread toward power among general society. Reports of mishaps including AC power added to these feelings of dread.

Interest in Mechanical Headways

Notwithstanding the panic based manipulation, the media's inclusion of electrical developments additionally provoked public curiosity in mechanical progressions. The commitment of electric lighting and the comfort it offered started interest and excitement.

Edison's Standing

Edison's dynamic commitment with the media and his painstakingly developed picture as a designer legend added to his standing as a solid and safe wellspring of electrical

innovation. The media's depiction of him as an irreplaceable asset reverberated with general society.

Tesla's Restricted Media Openness

Nikola Tesla's restricted media openness, joined with his whimsical thoughts, prompted a more specialty following. While certain lovers perceived his virtuoso, the more extensive public had a less clear comprehension of his commitments.

5. The Effect on Business and Industry

The media's depiction of the Conflict of Flows had direct ramifications for the business and industry.

Financial matters

Edison's supporting by lenders and financial matters prompted huge interests in DC power frameworks. These speculations were impacted to some extent by the media's depiction of Edison's DC as a protected and solid innovation.

Progress of AC Frameworks

In spite of the media's manipulating through scare tactics, the progress of AC frameworks, especially in significant distance power transmission, showed the specialized benefits of Tesla's creations. The media's job in molding general assessment didn't forestall the reception of AC innovation.

Inheritance and Authentic Reconsideration

In the years that followed, verifiable reconsideration and a more profound comprehension of Tesla's commitments prompted a change in open discernment. Tesla, when a moderately dark figure, earned respect as a splendid innovator whose developments changed electrical designing.

4.3 The role of key players, including George Westinghouse and J.P. Morgan, in this competition.

The late nineteenth century was a time of serious rivalry and development in the arising field of electric power. It was the point at which the world was progressing from gas and steam-based power frameworks to the progressive prospects presented by power. Two conspicuous figures who assumed significant parts in this change were George Westinghouse and J.P. Morgan. Each brought their one of a kind vision, assets, and impact to bear on the electric power scene, molding its course in significant ways. In this article, we will dig into the commitments of George Westinghouse and J.P. Morgan,

looking at what their activities meant for the improvement of electric power and its effect on society.

George Westinghouse: The Creator and Pioneer

George Westinghouse, brought into the world in 1846, was a creator and business person enthusiastically for designing. His initial developments incorporated the air powered brake, which upset the security and proficiency of the railroad business. In any case, it was Westinghouse's work in the field of electric power that would make a permanent imprint on history.

One of Westinghouse's most critical commitments was the turn of events and advancement of exchanging flow (AC) electrical frameworks. At that point, direct flow (DC) frameworks advocated by Thomas Edison were the prevailing type of electric power. Be that as it may, Westinghouse perceived the limits of DC, particularly over significant distances, and saw the likely in AC to defeat these difficulties.

Westinghouse's advancement accompanied his obtaining of the licenses for the air conditioner transformer and enlistment engine from

Nikola Tesla, another splendid innovator. These creations framed the underpinning of AC power dispersion. Westinghouse's vision was to utilize high-voltage AC to communicate power over significant distances prior to changing it to a lower voltage for safe use in homes and organizations. This approach offered a more functional and proficient arrangement than DC, particularly for enormous scope electrical frameworks.

One of the critical minutes in the fight among AC and DC came during the "Battle of Flows." Edison, supported by lenders like J.P. Morgan, enthusiastically went against AC, spreading fears of its alleged risk to human existence. Nonetheless, Westinghouse's tirelessness and the innate benefits of AC at last won. Quite, Westinghouse tied down an agreement to give AC capacity to the Chicago World's Fair in 1893, exhibiting the security and viability of the innovation to a huge number of guests.

J.P. Morgan: The Lender and Business Titan

J.P. Morgan, brought into the world in 1837, was a lender and broker who employed colossal impact over the American economy during the late nineteenth and mid twentieth hundreds of years. His association in the electric power contest was basically through his monetary advantages in the Edison General Electric Organization, which later converged with the Thomson-Houston Electric Organization to shape General Electric (GE).

Morgan was a big fan of Edison's DC power framework, which he accepted was the more secure and more dependable choice contrasted with Westinghouse's AC.

Morgan's monetary sponsorship and impact assisted Edison's organization with turning into a predominant player in the electric power industry.

The fight among AC and DC was not simply a mechanical one; it was likewise a business and monetary battle. Morgan, with his abundant resources and broad associations, assumed a significant part in supporting Edison's undertakings and advancing DC power. He utilized his monetary clout to get contracts for DC power frameworks, including the jolt of urban areas like New York and Philadelphia.

In any case, regardless of Morgan's endeavors, the intrinsic restrictions of DC power, especially its failure to be productively sent over significant distances, turned out to be progressively clear. This put Morgan and his Edison-supported drives in a tough spot as Westinghouse's AC framework showed its prevalence, particularly with regards to huge scope electrical dispersion.

The Consolidation and Result

In 1892, the electric power scene took a critical turn when Edison General Electric and Thomson-Houston Electric Organization, both upheld by compelling lenders like Morgan and Henry Villard, converged to frame General Electric (GE). This consolidation united the assets, licenses, and aptitude of two key part in the business.

General Electric, under the initiative of Charles Casket and Elihu Thomson, kept on creating both AC and DC hardware, perceiving the pragmatic uses of each. This undeniable an even minded shift in system, recognizing the benefits of AC while as yet taking special care of the current DC market.

The consolidation likewise denoted an essential second in the "Battle of Flows." With Edison's licenses now under a similar rooftop as Westinghouse's AC innovation, the competition among AC and DC turned out to be less extraordinary. General Electric's differentiated portfolio permitted it to stay a predominant power in the developing electric power industry, regardless of the flow type.

Inheritance and Effect

George Westinghouse's commitments to the electric power industry stretch out a long ways past the "Battle of Flows." His advancement of AC power frameworks established the groundwork for present day electrical networks, empowering the proficient transmission of power over significant distances. This improvement was instrumental in the zap of America and the world, controlling enterprises, homes, and urban areas.

Westinghouse's heritage additionally lives on through the Westinghouse Electric Company, which kept on enhancing in different fields, including atomic power. The

organization's work on atomic reactors and power plants lastingly affects the energy area.

J.P. Morgan's impact expanded well past the electric power industry, and his heritage stays huge in the monetary world. His help for Edison's undertakings, while eventually fruitless in the "Battle of Flows," mirrored his obligation to development and the organizations he put stock in.

Chapter 5

The Electric Chair Controversy

The hot seat, a grisly and questionable technique for execution, has been an image of both the quest for additional others conscious method for managing capital punishment and the moral situations encompassing the death penalty. Its development and reception in the late nineteenth century denoted a critical defining moment throughout the entire existence of execution strategies, setting off banters on the ethical quality, viability, and humankind of the hot seat as a type of the death penalty. In this complete investigation, we will dive into the hot seat discussion, analyzing its verifiable setting, its defenders and adversaries, and the getting through moral inquiries it raises.

1. **The Rise of the Hot seat**
   1.1 The Deadly Journey for a More Empathetic Execution Strategy
   In the nineteenth hundred years, as society wrestled with the morals of the death penalty and looked for additional others conscious options in contrast to customary techniques like hanging, a quest for a more edified type of execution picked up speed. The hot seat arose because of this journey for a strategy that sounds

apparent as not so much brutal but rather more logical.

1.2 The Clash of the Flows: AC versus DC

The innovation of the hot seat was intently attached to the "Battle of Flows" between Thomas Edison's immediate momentum (DC) and George Westinghouse's exchanging ebb and flow (AC) frameworks. The opposition between these two electrical frameworks had more extensive ramifications past the hot seat, however it assumed a huge part in the seat's turn of events.

2. The Introduction of the Hot seat

2.1 The Endeavors of Alfred P. Southwick

Dr. Alfred P. Southwick, a dental specialist with an interest in power, is frequently credited with proposing involving power for executions. He drew motivation from seeing coincidental passings brought about by electric shocks and accepted that power could offer an additional sympathetic and proficient method for completing capital punishments.

2.2 William Kemmler: The First to Face the Hot seat

William Kemmler, a sentenced killer, impacted the world forever in 1890 when he turned into the principal individual to be executed in the hot seat. The execution occurred in Reddish Jail in New York, denoting the start of the hot seat time.

3. The Discussion Encompassing the Hot seat

3.1 Ethical quality and Mankind

The hot seat promptly ignited extreme discussion over its ethical quality and mankind. That's what pundits contended, while it might have been more proficient, it was a horrifying and obtuse method for taking an individual's life. The grim idea of electric shocks, with witnesses frequently portraying stunning scenes of smoke, copying tissue, and delayed misery, just energized these worries.

3.2 Bungled Executions and Specialized Disappointments

The early utilization of the hot seat was damaged by a few messed up executions and specialized disappointments. These occurrences further increased the contention, bringing up issues about the dependability and sympathy of the strategy.

3.3 Legitimate Difficulties and Protected Questions

Legitimate difficulties to the hot seat emerged on numerous fronts, with adversaries contending that it abused the Eighth Amendment's preclusion against brutal and uncommon discipline. These provokes prompted critical court fights and discussions over the legality of electric shock.

4. The Hot seat Debate Across States

4.1 Reception by Different States

In spite of the discussions, numerous different states took on the hot seat as their favored technique for execution. It immediately turned into the most generally involved execution technique in the US, with the greater part of the states embracing it in the mid twentieth 100 years.

4.2 Popular Assessment and Abolitionist Developments

Popular assessment on the hot seat shifted broadly. While some saw it as an important innovative progression, others challenged its utilization, prompting the development of abolitionist developments devoted to finishing the death penalty by and large.

5. The Job of Prominent Figures in the Hot seat Discussion

5.1 George Westinghouse: A Hesitant Contribution

George Westinghouse, the air conditioner pioneer, found himself unintentionally attached to the hot seat discussion because of his association in the improvement of the exchanging flow framework. He communicated hesitance in regards to the utilization of power for executions and moved away from the affiliation.

5.2 Thomas Edison: Backing for the Hot seat

As opposed to Westinghouse, Thomas Edison upheld the hot seat for the purpose of advancing his DC electrical framework. He even ventured to such an extreme as to recommend that the demonstration of electric shock ought to be designated "Westing-housing" as a method for discoloring his rival's standing.

6. The Downfall of the Hot seat

6.1 The Ascent of Elective Execution Techniques

As the twentieth century advanced, elective techniques for execution, like deadly infusion, acquired ubiquity. These techniques were seen as more compassionate and less inclined to the specialized issues and abhorrent scenes related with the hot seat.

6.2 Enduring Moral Inquiries

The hot seat's decay didn't stop the moral inquiries encompassing capital punishment. The debate over the death penalty keeps on being a hostile issue, raising basic moral and lawful difficulties.

5.1Edison's involvement in promoting the electric chair for executions.

Thomas Edison, prestigious as perhaps of history's most noteworthy innovator, made significant commitments to the fields of power, lighting, and correspondence. Nonetheless, one of the hazier parts in his vocation includes his contribution in the advancement of the hot seat for the purpose of execution. Edison's promotion for the utilization of power in the death penalty originated from a blend of financial matters, logical interest, and a craving to ruin his rival, George Westinghouse. This exposition will investigate Edison's part in advancing the hot seat for executions, analyzing the inspirations driving his help and the results of his activities.

1. The Introduction of the Hot seat

1.1 The Journey for More Compassionate Execution Strategies

In the late nineteenth 100 years, society was progressively worried about the mercilessness and savagery of conventional execution techniques, like hanging and the

terminating crew. Advocates for change looked for elective method for managing capital punishment that sounds apparent as more altruistic, truly.

1.2 Edison's Contending Advantages

Thomas Edison was a trailblazer in the field of power. His advancement of the brilliant light and the advancement of direct flow (DC) electrical frameworks were extraordinary commitments to innovation and industry. In any case, Edison confronted tough opposition from George Westinghouse's exchanging flow (AC) electrical framework, which was more productive for communicating power over significant distances.

2. Edison's Association in the Hot seat

2.1 Edison's Resistance to Exchanging Current

Edison was a firm defender of direct current, which he considered to be better than exchanging current for most applications. As the "Battle of Flows" seethed between Edison's DC and Westinghouse's AC, Edison set out on a mission to dishonor AC, stressing its apparent risks and dangers.

2.2 The Chance to Ruin AC

Edison saw a chance to discolor the standing of AC by connecting it to the arising idea of involving power for executions. He trusted that by partner AC with the hot seat, he could influence general assessment against his rival's electrical framework.

3. The Advancement of the Hot seat

3.1 Edison's Help for the Hot seat

Edison effectively advanced the hot seat as a more sympathetic and proficient strategy for execution. He contended that it would be a quick and easy method for doing capital punishments, rather than the horrifying and frequently messed up hangings of the time.

3.2 The "Westinghousing" Idea

Edison ventured to such an extreme as to recommend that the demonstration of electric shock ought to be designated "Westinghousing," endeavoring to connect the cycle straightforwardly to his opponent, George Westinghouse. This move was important for Edison's more extensive work to harm the standing of AC by partner it with the detestations of the hot seat.

4. Edison's Job in the Improvement of the Hot seat

4.1 Counseling on the Plan

Edison gave specialized guidance and backing to those associated with planning the primary hot seat. His insight into electrical designing made him a significant asset in guaranteeing that the gadget would be proficient and solid.

4.2 William Kemmler: The Primary Casualty

The primary individual to be executed in the hot seat was William Kemmler, a sentenced killer. Kemmler's execution occurred on August 6, 1890, in Reddish Jail, New York. Edison's association in the advancement of the hot seat had arrived at its perfection with this occasion.

5. The Contention Encompassing Edison's Backing

5.1 Moral and Moral Inquiries

Edison's dynamic help for the hot seat brought up huge moral and moral issues. Pundits contended that his advancement of the technique for individual increase and to dishonor a contender was a critical and corrupt utilization of his impact.

5.2 Resistance and Public Objection

Edison's contribution in the hot seat discussion produced broad resistance and public clamor. Many saw his activities as insensitive and pioneering, discoloring his standing as a venerated creator and business person.

6. The Tradition of Edison's Contribution

6.1 The Downfall of the Hot seat

While Edison's association added to the underlying reception of the hot seat, the technique at last become undesirable. Deadly infusion, thought about a more others conscious other option, turned into the essential method for execution in many states.

6.2 The Continuous Discussion on The death penalty

Edison's support for the hot seat highlights the persevering through moral inquiries encompassing the death penalty. The discussion encompassing the technique mirrors the more extensive discussion on the ethical quality and mankind of capital punishment.

5.2 The ethical and moral debates surrounding the use of electricity for capital punishment.

The utilization of power for the death penalty, especially through the hot seat, has been the subject of serious moral and moral discussions since its origin in the late nineteenth hundred years. While defenders contend that it offers a more empathetic and productive

technique for execution, rivals raise worries about remorselessness, enduring, and the morals of state-endorsed killing. This paper investigates the complex moral and moral components of involving power for the death penalty, inspecting the contentions on the two sides and the getting through issues it presents.

1. **The Journey for More Altruistic Execution Strategies**
   1.1 Authentic Setting
   The historical backdrop of the death penalty is set apart by a constant journey for additional compassionate techniques for execution. Customary techniques, like hanging, decapitating, and terminating crews, were many times horrifying and excessively long undertakings, prompting a developing public clamor for change.
   1.2 The Development of Power
   As power arose as an extraordinary innovation in the late nineteenth hundred years, it raised the chance of an additional productive and apparently compassionate method for doing capital punishment. This time of trial and error saw the introduction of the hot seat as another technique for execution.
2. **Contentions For the Hot seat**
   2.1 Quick and Effortless Demise
   Defenders of the hot seat contend that it offers a faster and less

excruciating demise contrasted with customary strategies. They fight that the prompt use of a deadly electric flow instigates close momentary obviousness and heart failure, limiting torment.

2.2 Mechanical Advancement

Advocates likewise underscore the job of innovation in further developing execution strategies. They contend that the hot seat addresses progress in the organization of equity, lining up with the more extensive mechanical headways of the time.

3. Moral Worries and Resistance

3.1 Brutal and Strange Discipline

Adversaries of the hot seat fight that it comprises brutal and surprising discipline, which is restricted by the Eighth Amendment to the US Constitution. They highlight instances of messed up electric shocks, where the censured experienced delayed torment and anguishing passings.

3.2 The Exhibition of Death

Pundits contend that the hot seat propagates the shocking scene of execution, which can desensitize society to the demonstration of taking a human existence. The

perceivability of electric shocks, with witnesses frequently depicting the smell of consuming tissue and the horrifying idea of the interaction, brings up moral issues about the effect on witnesses and society at large.

4. The Job of Clinical Experts

4.1 Moral Issues for Clinical Staff

The association of clinical experts in managing the hot seat raises critical moral worries. Doctors and attendants who take part in executions might wind up in struggle with their expert vow to "cause no damage." Their job in causing demise, even at the command of the state, brings up issues about clinical morals and complicity in deadly demonstrations.

4.2 The Hippocratic Vow and Execution

The Hippocratic Vow, which numerous clinical experts stick to, unequivocally disallows support in executions. This pressure between proficient morals and state orders has prompted banters inside the clinical local area about the moral limits of their association.

5. The Apparition of Bungled Executions

5.1 The Gamble of Specialized Disappointments

The hot seat's set of experiences is defaced by cases of messed up executions because of specialized disappointments, including inappropriately aligned hardware and electrical floods. These occurrences have powered moral and moral worries about the dependability and adequacy of the technique.

5.2 The Enduring Injury

Overcomers of bungled electric shocks frequently experience extreme physical and mental injury. These cases bring up issues about the obligation of the state in causing mischief and enduring, even unexpectedly, during the execution cycle.

6. The Effect on Witnesses and Society

6.1 Observer Injury

The observers to hot seat executions, including jail staff, relatives of the person in question, and media delegates, can encounter significant injury and mental pain. Seeing the abhorrences of electric shocks can have durable profound and moral outcomes.

6.2 Desensitization to Brutality

The rehashed openness to executions, especially through the hot seat, can desensitize society to the demonstration of taking a human existence. This desensitization raises moral worries about the debasement of human existence and the potential for a general public that is more tolerating of viciousness.

7. The Worldwide Viewpoint

7.1 Global Abolitionist Developments

Numerous nations all over the planet have nullified the utilization of the hot seat and the death penalty out and out. The global local area, through associations like Reprieve Worldwide, has supported for the annulment of capital punishment on the grounds of basic freedoms and moral contemplations.

7.2 The US's Fluctuated Approach

In the US, the utilization of the hot seat shifts from one state to another. A few states have nullified it for other execution strategies, like deadly infusion, while others keep on utilizing it. This interwoven methodology mirrors the continuous moral and moral discussions encompassing the death penalty.

5.3 The impact of the electric chair controversy on the public's perception of electricity.

The hot seat debate, which arose in the late nineteenth hundred years for the purpose of controlling capital punishment, significantly affected the public's view of power. At the point when power was an image of progress and advancement, its relationship with the frightful demonstration of execution in the hot seat raised complex moral, moral, and social inquiries. This article digs into the manners by which the hot seat discussion molded the public's impression of power, impacting how society saw this extraordinary innovation.

1. **Power as an Image of Progress**
   1.1 The Rise of Power
   In the late nineteenth 100 years, power was an image of mechanical headway and innovation. It had changed businesses, enlightened urban communities, and was viewed as a main impetus behind monetary and social advancement.
   1.2 Power's Positive Affiliations
   Power was related with positive improvements like the electric light, telecommunication, and electric trolleys. It was seen as a spotless and effective energy source that could work on individuals' lives and drive development.
2. **The Introduction of the Hot seat**
   2.1 The "Battle of Flows"

The contention between Thomas Edison's immediate current (DC) and George Westinghouse's substituting current (AC) frameworks, known as the "Battle of Flows," was at its top during this period. Both Edison and Westinghouse looked to lay out their electrical frameworks as the predominant type of zap.

2.2 The Hot seat as a Disputable Development

The hot seat, created for the purpose of execution by power, turned into a questionable image at the convergence of innovation, morals, and equity. It tested the view of power as a power for good and raised worries about its possible abuse.

3. The Effect on Open Insight

3.1 Power as a Situation with two sides

The hot seat introduced power as a situation with two sides. While it displayed the potential for power to be bridled for life changing headways, it additionally featured its disastrous limit when utilized for the death penalty.

3.2 The Horrifying Side of Power

The hot seat debate uncovered the clouded side of power. Realistic portrayals of electric shocks, with witnesses frequently revealing horrifying scenes of smoke, copying tissue, and enduring, made a distinct difference with the positive picture of power as a groundbreaking power.

4. Moral and Moral Problems

4.1 Public Discussion and Objection

The hot seat contention started serious public discussions about the morals of involving power for executions. Papers and public gatherings were loaded up with conversations on the ethical ramifications of the technique, prompting boundless public objection.

4.2 Brutal and Surprising Discipline

Pundits contended that the hot seat comprised brutal and surprising discipline, bringing up issues about the profound quality of utilizing an innovation related with progress to do capital punishments.

5. The Effect on Writing and Mainstream society

5.1 Abstract Works

The hot seat discussion tracked down its direction into writing, with writers investigating the moral and moral components of the issue. Works like "The Green Mile" by Stephen Ruler and "Doomed soul" by Sister Helen Prejean dug into the intricacies of the hot seat for the purpose of execution.

5.2 Media and Diversion

The hot seat discussion likewise left an enduring engraving on mainstream society. Films, TV programs, and narratives have portrayed the repulsions of the hot seat, further solidifying its relationship with remorselessness and languishing.

6. Lawful and Authoritative Repercussions

6.1 Court Difficulties

The moral and moral discussions encompassing the hot seat prompted lawful difficulties. Adversaries contended that it abused the Eighth Amendment's disallowance against savage and uncommon discipline, prompting critical court fights.

6.2 Changes in Execution Strategies

Because of the debate, a few states in the US started to get rid of the hot seat for other execution techniques, for example, deadly infusion, which were seen as more compassionate.

7. The Continuous Effect

7.1 The Tradition of the Hot seat Contention

The hot seat discussion's inheritance perseveres, filling in as a sign of the mind boggling transaction between innovation, morals, and society. It has left an enduring engraving on the public's impression of power, featuring the ethical issues related with its utilization in different settings.

7.2 The death penalty Discussions

The hot seat discussion has likewise added to continuous discussions about the death penalty. It highlights the moral inquiries encompassing capital punishment and the strategies used to do it.

|94|

Chapter 6

The Battle for Niagara Falls

Niagara Falls, situated on the boundary between the US and Canada, is perhaps of the most spectacular normal miracle on the planet. The sheer size and force of these falls have caught human creative mind for a really long time, and they have likewise been the focal point of an alternate sort of battle — a fight not so much for command an over area, but rather for command over the falls' tremendous hydroelectric potential.

This exposition investigates the captivating history of the Fight for Niagara Falls, a contention that set ecological protection in opposition to modern turn of events, public interests against worldwide partici-pation, and the safeguarding of regular excellence against the age of electrical power. Throughout the twentieth hundred years, the battle to saddle Niagara's power significantly affects the locale, molded the ad-vancement of hydroelectric innovation, and presented significant moral and natural inquiries.

1. **The Force of Niagara Falls**
   1.1 Regular Marvel and Vacation spot
   Niagara Falls comprises of three principal cascades: the Horseshoe

Falls, the American Falls, and the Marriage Cover Falls. These falls by and large produce a stunning exhibition, drawing a huge number of sightseers from around the world to observe their excellence and power.

1.2 Early Acknowledgment of Hydroelectric Potential

The possibility to bridle the motor energy of the succumbs to power age was perceived as soon as the nineteenth 100 years. Designers and specialists started to investigate the plausibility of taking advantage of this uncommon regular asset to fulfill the developing need for electrical power.

2. The Beginning of the Hydroelectric Time

2.1 Nikola Tesla and Rotating Current

The advancement of exchanging flow (AC) electrical frameworks, advocated by Nikola Tesla and upheld by George Westinghouse, upset the transmission of power over significant distances. AC's proficiency made it especially appropriate for tackling the force of Niagara Falls.

2.2 The Development of the Niagara Falls Power Organization

In 1886, the Niagara Falls Power Organization was laid out to seek after the aggressive objective of tackling the succumbs to power age. It denoted the start of another period in hydroelectric power advancement.

3. The Underlying Fight: Exchanging Current versus Direct Current

3.1 The "Battle of Flows"

The "Battle of Flows" between advocates of substituting flow (AC), like Tesla and Westinghouse, and allies of direct flow (DC), drove by Thomas Edison and General Electric, worked out at Niagara Falls. The result of this fight would shape the fate of electrical power age.

3.2 AC Wins at Niagara

Eventually, AC won at Niagara Falls because of its capacity to productively communicate power over significant distances. The jolt of Bison, New York, in 1896 denoted the outcome of AC power age at the falls and an achievement throughout the entire existence of hydroelectricity.

4. **The Global Joint Commission and Settlement of 1909**
4.1 Worldwide Strategy
The Niagara Stream, which takes care of Niagara Falls, shapes a characteristic line between the US and Canada. Perceiving the global ramifications of outfitting the falls' power, the two countries laid out the Worldwide Joint Commission (IJC) to regulate the common asset.

4.2 The Arrangement of 1909
The Arrangement of 1909 reaffirmed the responsibility of the two nations to the economical improvement of Niagara Falls. It laid out unambiguous arrangements for the designation of water privileges and power age, underlining worldwide participation and natural protection.

5. **The Development of the Power Plants**
5.1 The Sir Adam Beck Hydroelectric Power Stations
In Canada, the Sir Adam Beck Hydroelectric Power Stations, named after an unmistakable legislator, were developed along the Niagara Waterway in the mid twentieth hundred years. These plants contributed fundamentally to power age and became notorious images of hydroelectric power.

5.2 The Robert Moses Niagara Power Plant
On the American side, the Robert Moses Niagara Power Plant, named after the persuasive public authority Robert Moses, was worked to bridle the falls' energy. It remains as a demonstration of designing ability and the desire of taking advantage of this regular asset.

6. **Natural and Moral Worries**
6.1 The Effect on the Falls' Style
The development of force plants and the redirection of water for

hydroelectric purposes prompted worries about the visual effect on the falls. Pundits contended that the controlled progression of water decreased the regular excellence of Niagara.

6.2 Biological Ramifications

The Fight for Niagara Falls additionally raised biological worries. Changes to the progression of the stream and the development of force plants could disturb the regular environment and relocation examples of amphibian species.

7. Protection and The travel industry

7.1 Protection Endeavors

As worries developed over the effect of force age on the falls, protection endeavors picked up speed. Associations and people attempted to safeguard and reestablish the regular magnificence of Niagara Falls.

7.2 The travel industry and Financial Effect

In spite of the progressions achieved by power age, the travel industry stayed a flourishing industry. The falls kept on drawing guests, contributing fundamentally to the territorial economy and showing the way that the safeguarding of regular magnificence and monetary improvement could coincide.

8. The Advanced Period: Manageable Hydroelectric Power

8.1 Advances in Hydroelectric Innovation

The hydroelectric power industry has advanced altogether since its beginning at Niagara Falls. Progresses in innovation, including more proficient turbines and natural observing frameworks, have empowered more supportable power age.

8.2 Adjusting Energy Needs and Protection

The Fight for Niagara Falls fills in as a contextual analysis in the continuous test of offsetting energy needs with ecological preservation. Today, endeavors are being made

to moderate the natural effect of hydroelectric power age while satisfying the developing need for clean energy.

6.1 The iconic competition to harness the power of Niagara Falls.

Niagara Falls, a characteristic marvel situated on the boundary between the US and Canada, has enamored the creative mind of millions with its stunning excellence and massive power. The narrative of saddling Niagara Falls' power is a story of resourcefulness, contest, and the determined quest for innovative headway. This notable rivalry, which unfurled in the late nineteenth and mid twentieth hundreds of years, denoted a crucial crossroads throughout the entire existence of hydro-electric power age and has left an enduring heritage. In this article, we investigate the sensational rivalry to saddle the force of Niagara Falls, analyzing the vital participants, mechanical developments, and the expansive effect of this notable undertaking.

1. **The Superbness of Niagara Falls**

   1.1 A Characteristic Miracle

   Niagara Falls comprises of three essential cascades: the Horseshoe Falls, the American Falls, and the Wedding Shroud Falls. The joined volume of water that streams over the falls makes it quite possibly of the most remarkable cascade on the planet, drawing in travelers and explorers the same.

   1.2 Early Acknowledgment of Potential

   Early guests to Niagara Falls perceived its true capacity for creating energy. The falls' dynamic energy was apparent, and designers and architects started to investigate ways of bridling this energy for different purposes.

2. **The Coming of Power**

   2.1 Rise of Electrical Power

   The late nineteenth century saw the quick turn of events and reception of electrical power as an extraordinary innovation. Advancements in electrical designing and the improvement of electrical frameworks set up for the opposition to bridle Niagara Falls' power for power age.

   2.2 The Clash of the Flows

The contention between direct current (DC), supported by Thomas Edison, and substituting current (AC), advanced by George Westinghouse and Nikola Tesla, turned into a characterizing component of the opposition. The result would decide the fate of electrical power transmission.

3. **Central participants in the Opposition**

3.1 Thomas Edison: Defender of Direct Current

Thomas Edison, a productive creator, and finance manager, was a resolute backer for direct flow (DC) electrical frameworks. He accepted DC was the more secure and more solid choice for power dispersion.

3.2 George Westinghouse: Promoter for Substituting Current

George Westinghouse, an industrialist and designer, supported substituting current (AC) frameworks. He accepted AC was more proficient for communicating power over significant distances, making it reasonable for saddling Niagara Falls' power.

3.3 Nikola Tesla: AC's Specialized Trailblazer

Nikola Tesla, an electrical designer and creator, made huge commitments to the improvement of AC electrical frameworks. His creations and licenses assumed a significant part in the outcome of AC power age.

4. **The Development of the Niagara Falls Power Organization**

4.1 The Visionaries

In 1886, a gathering of visionaries established the Niagara Falls Power Organization. Their objective was aggressive: to outfit the force of Niagara Succumbs to power age on an uncommon scale.

4.2 The Aggressive Objective

The Niagara Falls Power Organization intended to fabricate a framework fit for communicating power over significant distances to significant urban communities like Bison and New York City. This vision required conquering huge specialized and strategic difficulties.

5. **The Conflict of Flows at Niagara Falls**

5.1 Edison's Resistance to AC

Thomas Edison enthusiastically went against the reception of rotating current for the Niagara Falls project. He took incredible measures to ruin AC, in any event, leading public showings of the risks of high-voltage AC power.

5.2 AC Wins at Niagara

Notwithstanding Edison's endeavors, substituting current won at Niagara Falls. George Westinghouse's AC framework was picked for the amazing errand of sending power from the tumbles to far off metropolitan communities.

6. **The Development of the Principal Power Plants**

6.1 The Edward Senior member Adams Power Plant

The Edward Senior member Adams Power Plant, built at Niagara Falls, was the principal major hydroelectric power station. It denoted the start of huge scope power age utilizing the falls' power.

6.2 The Approach of Transmission Lines

To understand the aggressive objective of sending power over significant distances, engineers grew high-voltage transmission lines, exhibiting the plausibility of communicating power from Niagara Tumbles to metropolitan focuses.

7. **The Effect of Niagara Falls Hydroelectric Power**

7.1 Charge of Bison

In 1896, Bison, New York, became quite possibly the earliest city to profit from the power created at Niagara Falls. The charge of Bison denoted an achievement throughout the entire existence of hydroelectric power age.

7.2 The Change of Industry

The accessibility of bountiful and reasonable electrical power from Niagara Falls prodded modern development and advancement. Businesses going from assembling to substance handling tackled this recently discovered energy source to fuel their activities.

8. Moral and Natural Ramifications

8.1 Preservation Concerns

The change of Niagara Falls into a hydroelectric power source brought up moral issues about the likely effect on the falls' regular excellence. Preservationists voiced worries about the ecological and tasteful outcomes of force age.

8.2 The Arrangement of 1909

Perceiving the requirement for mindful turn of events, the US and Canada marked the Deal of 1909. This settlement laid out arrangements for the designation of water freedoms and power age at Niagara Falls, underlining collaboration and protection.

9. Heritage and Continuous Hydroelectric Turn of events

9.1 The Getting through Heritage

The opposition to bridle Niagara Falls' power left a getting through inheritance. It exhibited the potential for hydroelectric power age and set up for additional headways in environmentally friendly power innovation.

9.2 Present day Hydroelectric Turn of events

Today, Niagara Falls keeps on producing hydroelectric power, with present day plants working on both the American and Canadian sides. Progresses in innovation and natural mindfulness have prompted more manageable power age rehearses.

6.2How Tesla's AC system triumphed over Edison's DC in the Niagara Falls project.

The Niagara Falls project denoted a vital crossroads throughout the entire existence of electrical power age. It was a landmark where two titans of development, Thomas Edison and George Westinghouse, supported contending electrical frameworks: direct flow (DC) and exchanging flow (AC). In this exposition, we dig into how Nikola Tesla's AC framework eventually won over Edison's DC in the Niagara Falls project. We investigate the mechanical developments, the crucial job of Tesla, and the sweeping results of this fight in the advancement of electrical designing and power age.

1. **The Ascent of Electrical Power**

   1.1 Rise of Electrical Frameworks

   At the turn of the twentieth 100 years, the reception of electrical power was changing ventures, urban communities, and families. Power offered uncommon open doors for development and progress, yet it likewise ignited serious contest among innovators and industrialists.

   1.2 Edison's Immediate Current (DC) Framework

   Thomas Edison, celebrated for designing the brilliant light, supported the immediate flow (DC) electrical framework. DC was the predominant innovation at that point, however it had impediments, especially in significant distance transmission.

2. **Exchanging Current (AC) and the Virtuoso of Nikola Tesla**

   2.1 Nikola Tesla: A Visionary Creator

   Nikola Tesla, a Serbian-conceived creator and electrical specialist, was a splendid and whimsical scholar. His work established the groundwork for the reception of substituting flow (AC) as a practical electrical framework.

   2.2 Tesla's Commitment to AC Innovation

   Tesla made basic commitments to AC innovation, including the improvement of the air conditioner engine, transformer, and polyphase framework. These creations reformed electrical power transmission, making it conceivable to send power proficiently over significant distances.

3. **The Fight for Niagara Falls**

   3.1 The Niagara Falls Power Organization

   The Niagara Falls Power Organization was shaped in 1886 with the aggressive objective of bridling Niagara Falls' ability to produce power for a huge scope. This venture turned into a point of convergence in the fight among DC and AC.

3.2 Edison's Resistance to AC

Thomas Edison, a defender of DC, energetically went against the utilization of rotating current for the Niagara Falls project. He directed a mission to dishonor AC, in any event, organizing public showings of its apparent risks.

4. The Air conditioner Benefit

4.1 AC's Effectiveness in Transmission

One of the vital benefits of AC over DC was its proficiency in significant distance transmission. AC voltage could be handily changed to sequential levels utilizing Tesla's advancements, permitting power to be moved over huge distances without critical misfortune.

4.2 Westinghouse's Reception of AC

George Westinghouse, an industrialist and designer, perceived the capability of AC for the Niagara Falls project. He got Tesla's licenses and mastery, pursuing AC the favored decision for the improvement of the electrical framework at the falls.

5. The Jolt of Bison

5.1 The Meaning of Bison

Bison, New York, filled in as a proving ground for the transmission of power produced at Niagara Falls. The zap of Bison was a critical second in showing the possibility of AC for significant distance power transmission.

5.2 AC Wins at Bison

In 1896, Bison became perhaps the earliest city on the planet to be controlled by power created at a far off hydroelectric plant. The outcome of AC transmission from Niagara Tumbles to Bison was a demonstration of Tesla's developments and Westinghouse's vision.

6. The Conflict of Flows Settled

6.1 The Decay of DC

As AC innovation showed its prevalence in reasonable applications, DC started to melt away in notoriety. The progress of the

Niagara Falls project denoted a defining moment in the "Battle of Flows," setting AC as the prevailing electrical framework for power age and transmission.

6.2 Tradition of the Niagara Falls Undertaking

The Niagara Falls venture's prosperity significantly affected the fate of electrical designing and power age. AC turned into the norm for electrical frameworks, empowering the far and wide charge of urban areas and ventures.

7. The Proceeding with Effect of AC

7.1 The Air conditioner Power Lattice

The reception of AC innovation prompted the improvement of the advanced electrical power matrix. This interconnected arrangement of force age, transmission, and dissemination reformed energy access and changed society.

7.2 Tesla's Getting through Inheritance

Nikola Tesla's commitments to electrical designing keep on forming the world. His developments and advancements in AC innovation established the groundwork for present day electrical frameworks, and his vision of remote power transmission stays an area of continuous examination and investigation.

6.3 The pivotal moment in the transition to AC as the standard for power distribution.

The progress from direct flow (DC) to substituting flow (AC) as the norm for power circulation was a significant crossroads throughout the entire existence of electrical designing and energy transmission. This change, which unfurled in the late nineteenth and mid twentieth hundreds of years, generally reshaped how power was produced, sent, and used. In this article, we investigate the critical variables and occasions that prompted the domination of AC, analyzing the commitments of designers like Nikola Tesla and the significant effect of this change on society and innovation.

1. **The Beginning of Electrical Power**
   1.1 The Rise of Electrical Frameworks
   The late nineteenth century saw the ascent of electrical power as a progressive innovation. Early analyses with power established the groundwork for the improvement
   of electrical frameworks that could be saddled for lighting, transportation, and modern applications.
   1.2 Edison's Immediate Current (DC) Framework
   Thomas Edison, a commended designer and business visionary, supported the immediate flow (DC) electrical framework. DC was the predominant innovation in the beginning phases of electrical power, however it had inborn limits, especially with respect to productive significant distance transmission.

2. **The Contention of Electrical Flows**
   2.1 The "Battle of Flows"
   The contention between defenders of DC and AC, frequently alluded to as the "Battle of Flows," turned into a characterizing component of the progress. Thomas Edison was a resolute backer for DC, while George Westinghouse and Nikola Tesla supported AC.
   2.2 Edison's Resistance to AC
   Thomas Edison overwhelmingly went against the reception of substituting current for power transmission. He led a mission to ruin AC, in any event, organizing public exhibitions to feature its apparent risks.

3. **Tesla's Vision and AC Benefits**
   3.1 Nikola Tesla: The Visionary Innovator
   Nikola Tesla, a Serbian-conceived creator and electrical specialist, arose as a critical figure in the change to AC. His eccentric reasoning and imaginative commitments would assume a urgent part in AC's power.
   3.2 Tesla's AC Commitments
   Tesla made huge commitments to AC innovation, including the

advancement of the air conditioner engine, transformer, and polyphase framework. These innovations altered electrical power transmission, making it attainable to communicate power proficiently over significant distances.

4. **The Charge of Bison**

   4.1 Bison as a Proving Ground

   Bison, New York, filled in as a proving ground for the transmission of power produced at remote power plants. The jolt of Bison assumed an essential part in exhibiting the possibility and effectiveness of AC for significant distance power circulation.

   4.2 AC's Victory in Bison

   In 1896, Bison became one of the main urban communities worldwide to be controlled by power produced at a distant hydroelectric plant utilizing AC transmission. This achievement was a demonstration of the benefits of AC innovation and denoted a huge defining moment in the change.

5. **The Effect on Electrical Designing**

   5.1 Change of Electrical Designing

   The progress to AC as the norm for power dissemination significantly affected electrical designing. It prompted the advancement of additional proficient electrical frameworks and innovations, powering further developments in the field.

   5.2 Expansion of Electrical Frameworks

   The far and wide reception of AC power appropriation took into consideration the charge of urban communities, enterprises, and families on a phenomenal scale. This change raised expectations for everyday comforts, worked with modern development, and drove monetary turn of events.

6. **Present day AC Power Frameworks**

   6.1 The Air conditioner Power Framework

   The improvement of the advanced electrical power matrix, in light of AC innovation, altered energy access and use. The interconnected arrangement of force age, transmission, and appropriation changed how power was created and conveyed.

6.2 Tesla's Getting through Heritage

Nikola Tesla's commitments to AC innovation keep on molding the world. His developments and advancements established the groundwork for current electrical frameworks, and his visionary thoughts, like remote power transmission, remain subjects of progressing examination and investigation.

7. Moral and Natural Ramifications

7.1 Manageable Power Conveyance

The change to AC power circulation likewise had moral and natural ramifications. AC's proficiency in significant distance transmission made it conceivable to tackle energy from remote, frequently sustainable sources, lessening the natural effect of force age.

7.2 The Job of Preservation

The shift towards AC power circulation highlighted the significance of preservation and effective energy use. As electrical frameworks turned out to be more far reaching, society progressively perceived the requirement for capable energy utilization.

Chapter 7

The Inventors' Personal Lives

In the chronicles of history, creators and trend-setters stand as transcending figures who have molded the world with their manifestations and disclosures. While their developments have frequently been the focal point of consideration, the individual existences of these striking people are similarly captivating. This paper digs into the individual existences of a few noticeable designers, investigating their experiences, difficulties, connections, and the unpredictable transaction between their own encounters and their weighty work.

1. Thomas Edison: The Wizard of Menlo Park

1.1 Early Life and Training

Thomas Edison, known as the "Wizard of Menlo Park," was brought into the world in 1847 in Milan, Ohio. His initial training was humble, yet his curious nature and independent learning established the groundwork for his future developments.

1.2 Family and Individual Difficulties

Edison's own life was set apart by various difficulties, including hearing impedance since the beginning. In spite of these obstacles, he drove forward and became quite possibly of the most productive designer ever.

1.3 Connections and Conjugal Life

Edison's most memorable union with Mary Stilwell finished unfortunately with her passing in 1884. He later wedded Mina Mill operator, and their association delivered three youngsters. Edison's devotion to his work frequently stressed his day to day life, however he remained profoundly dedicated to his better half and kids.

2. Nikola Tesla: The Visionary Virtuoso

2.1 Early Years and Schooling

Nikola Tesla, a Serbian-American designer, was brought into the world in 1856 in current Croatia. His initial instruction and childhood underlined designing and science, giving areas of strength for a to his future work.

2.2 The Unconventional Virtuoso

Tesla was known for his erraticisms and offbeat way of behaving. His serious spotlight on his work at times practically ruled out private connections, and he stayed unmarried all through his life.

2.3 Battles with Funds

In spite of his brightness, Tesla confronted monetary difficulties all through his vocation. His fixation on his work, combined with unfortunate business choices, prompted monetary shakiness and times of destitution.

3. Alexander Graham Chime: The Designer of the Phone

3.1 Early Life and Family

Alexander Graham Chime, brought into the world in 1847 in Scotland, was profoundly affected by his family's advantage in address and discourse. His mom and spouse, Mabel Gardiner Hubbard, assumed huge parts in his day to day existence and work.

3.2 The Phone and Hard of hearing Instruction

Chime's development of the phone was intently attached to his work with the hard of hearing local area. He gave himself to further developing correspondence for the consultation weakened and assumed a urgent part in the foundation of the American Phone and Transmit Organization (AT&T).

3.3 Family and Individual Misfortunes

Chime's own life was set apart by wins and misfortunes. He lost two children to early passings, and his dedication to his work now and again stressed his associations with relatives. All things considered, his family stayed a wellspring of motivation.

4. **Marie Curie: The Trailblazer in Radioactivity**

4.1 Early Years and Instruction

Marie Curie, brought into the world in 1867 in Warsaw, Poland, showed an early fitness for science and math. Her devotion to her examinations prompted her spearheading research in radio-activity.

4.2 The Nobel Laureate Curie's pivotal work in radioactivity procured her two Nobel Prizes — one in Physical science and one in Science. Her accomplishments broke orientation obstructions in science and the scholarly community.

4.3 Individual Penances

Curie's commitment to her work came at an individual expense. Her openness to radiation during her exploration probably added to her medical problems and possible demise. She likewise confronted public examination and contention because of her unusual individual life, incorporating her relationship with individual researcher Pierre Curie.

5. **Albert Einstein: The Relativity Virtuoso**

5.1 Early Life and Schooling

Albert Einstein, brought into the world in 1879 in Ulm, Germany, exhibited early indications of scholarly splendor. His schooling and childhood supported his interest and love for ma-terial science.

5.2 The Hypothesis of Relativity

Einstein's hypothesis of relativity upset material science and acquired him global recognition. His own life, nonetheless, was set apart by intricacies and connections that mirrored his novel perspective.

5.3 Individual Convictions and Social Activism

Einstein was known for his conservative convictions and social activism. He utilized his distinction to advocate for harmony, social liberties, and philanthropic causes, making him a logical symbol as well as a worldwide figure of soul.

6. Ada Lovelace: The World's Most memorable Software engineer

6.1 The Little girl of Ruler Byron

Augusta Ada Lord, Royal lady of Lovelace, known as Ada Lovelace, was brought into the world in 1815 in London, Britain. She was the little girl of the renowned artist Master Byron and mathematician Annabella Milbanke.

6.2 Cooperation with Charles Babbage

Lovelace is most popular for her work with Charles Babbage, who planned the Logical Motor, an early mechanical PC. Lovelace's notes on the motor contained the principal distributed calculation expected for execution on a PC, procuring her the title of the world's most memorable software engineer.

6.3 Individual Battles and Wellbeing

Lovelace's own life was set apart by wellbeing battles, remembering persistent diseases and a reliance for laudanum. Regardless of these difficulties, her spearheading work in

PC programming left an enduring inheritance.

7.1A glimpse into the personal lives and contrasting personalities of Edison and Tesla.

The late nineteenth and mid twentieth hundreds of years were a period of incredible development and logical disclosure, and two of the most unmistakable figures of this time were Thomas Edison and Nikola Tesla. While the two men made critical commitments to the universe of science and innovation, they had boundlessly unique individual lives and differentiating characters. This exposition will give a brief look into the individual existences of these two incredible designers, featuring the novel characteristics that put them aside.

Thomas Edison, frequently alluded to as the "Wizard of Menlo Park," was brought into the world on February 11, 1847, in Milan, Ohio. He was the seventh and most youthful kid in his loved ones. Edison's experience growing up was set apart by a progression of difficulties and mishaps. He battled with hearing issues since the beginning, which made it hard for him to successfully convey. This consultation weakness, in any case, didn't hinder him from seeking after his enthusiasm for trial and error and creation.

Edison's own life was described by his steady hard working attitude and a guarantee to his logical interests. He was known for working extended periods, frequently keeping awake during that time to direct investigations and create new gadgets. Edison's commitment to his work practically ruled out a traditional everyday life. He was hitched two times, first to Mary Stilwell in 1871, with whom he had three youngsters, and later to Mina Mill operator in 1886, with whom he had three additional kids. In spite of his family responsibilities, Edison kept on focusing on his work, which now and again stressed his connections.

Conversely, Nikola Tesla, brought into the world on July 10, 1856, in Smiljan, Croatia, had a boundlessly unique childhood and individual life. Tesla came from a Serbian family and was the fourth of five kids. His dad was a Serbian Standard minister, and his mom impacted his initial schooling and childhood. Tesla showed a surprising fitness for math and science since early on, and his folks perceived his gifts and energized his scholarly interests.

Tesla's own life was set apart by his unconventionalities and hermitic nature. Not at all like Edison, who was a well known person known for his various developments and licenses, Tesla was to a greater degree a lone designer who frequently minded his own business. He never wedded or had youngsters and dedicated as long as he can remember to his logical work. Tesla's hard working attitude was no less thorough than

Edison's, yet his way to deal with life was more plain and zeroed in exclusively on his logical undertakings.

One of the most striking differentiations among Edison and Tesla was their way to deal with creation and advancement. Edison was a down to earth designer who had confidence in experimentation. He broadly said, "I have not fizzled. I've quite recently found 10,000 different ways that won't work." Edison's methodology included efficient trial and error, and he held various licenses for innovations going from the phonograph to the electric light. His innovations were frequently outfitted towards useful applications and working on the regular routines of conventional individuals.

Tesla, then again, was a visionary creator with an emphasis on hypothetical and logical standards. He had a profound comprehension of material science and math and frequently ironed out the subtleties of his developments to him before truly constructing a model. Tesla's innovations, like exchanging flow (AC) electrical frameworks and the Tesla loop, were more unique and significantly affected the field of electrical designing. His work established the groundwork for the vast majority current advances, including remote correspondence and radio.

One more key distinction among Edison and Tesla was their way to deal with business and commercialization. Edison was a canny money manager who established General Electric (GE) and was effectively engaged with showcasing and advancing his innovations. He figured out the significance of licenses and protected innovation and involved them for his potential benefit in the business world. Edison's innovative soul permitted him to accumulate impressive abundance during his lifetime.

Tesla, then again, was less intrigued by monetary profit and more centered around the quest for information. He frequently battled monetarily and was not as skilled at commercializing his innovations. While Tesla held various licenses, he offered a portion of his patent privileges to financial backers, which eventually left him with restricted monetary assets. Tesla's needs were solidly established in progressing logical seeing as opposed to amassing abundance.

As far as character, Edison was known for his constancy and assurance. He was a persevering issue solver who was not effortlessly deterred by disappointment. His adage, "Virtuoso is 1% motivation and close to 100% sweat," mirrors his faith in the significance of difficult work and determination. Edison was likewise a self-advertiser and knew how to catch the public's creative mind with his innovations and exhibits.

Tesla, then again, was a more cryptic and contemplative figure. He was known for his erratic ways of behaving and propensities. Tesla had areas of strength for a to

microorganisms and was known to fanatically clean his eating table and flatware. He additionally professed to have surprising dreams and encounters, which added to his persona. Tesla's hermitic nature and unconventional ways of behaving added to the view of him as a "crazy lab rat" in mainstream society.

Regardless of their disparities, Edison and Tesla made huge commitments to the universe of science and innovation. Edison's innovations changed the manner in which we live, with the electric light, phonograph, and films becoming necessary pieces of current life. Tesla's work on AC power and remote correspondence laid the basis for the advanced electrical network and the improvement of radio and TV.

7.2 Their relationships, struggles, and personal challenges.

Thomas Edison and Nikola Tesla, two of history's most celebrated designers, not just made a permanent imprint on the universe of science and innovation yet in addition had rich and complex individual lives loaded up with connections, battles, and individual difficulties. This article dives into the mind boggling embroidery of their lives, investigating the elements of their connections, the impressive snags they confronted, and the interesting individual difficulties that characterized their inheritances.

Thomas Edison's Connections and Battles

Thomas Edison's life was set apart by a progression of individual and expert connections, some of which were strong, while others presented huge difficulties.

1. **Edison's Loved ones:** Edison's day to day life was one of blended favors. He wedded Mary Stilwell in 1871, and they had three kids together. Notwithstanding, misfortune struck when Mary passed on in 1884. Edison battled to adjust his requesting work plan with his family obligations. His second union with Mina Mill operator in 1886 carried a soundness to his own life, and they had three kids. Notwithstanding his familial responsibilities, Edison's determined hard working attitude frequently outweighed everything else, stressing his associations with his spouses and youngsters.

2. **Proficient Connections:** Edison's expert connections were similarly mind boggling. His nearby coordinated effort with creators and specialists like Charles Batchelor and Francis Upton was significant to his prosperity. In any case, his way to deal with collaboration was not agreeable all the time. Edison was known for his requesting and some of the time despotic authority style, which caused grinding with a portion of his partners. His contention with Nikola Tesla, for instance, was set apart by serious rivalry and a conspicuous difference in ways to deal with electrical designing, prompting stressed relations between the two creators.

3. **Patent Conflicts:** Edison was entangled in various patent debates all through his profession, generally outstandingly the "Battle of the Flows" with George Westinghouse, a fight over the reception of exchanging flow (AC) versus direct flow (DC) for power conveyance. These fights in court were monetarily depleting as well as genuinely burdening for Edison.

4. **The Deficiency of Hearing:** Quite possibly of the main individual test Edison confronted was his slow loss of hearing, which started in youth. As his hearing decayed, Edison turned out to be progressively confined, prompting challenges in correspondence and social cooperations. Regardless of this impediment, he proceeded to enhance and imagine, depending on his instinct and persistence to beat the constraints of his hearing debilitation.

Nikola Tesla's Connections and Battles

Nikola Tesla, rather than Edison, had a more singular existence, frequently focusing on his work over private connections. His encounters were shaded by an alternate arrangement of difficulties and connections.

1. **Absence of Individual Connections:** Tesla was a long lasting unhitched male and had no known heartfelt or familial connections. His dedication to his work and his isolated nature made it trying for him to shape special interactions. Tesla's nearest connections were frequently with his pigeons, whom he really focused on and took care of day to day, prompting hypothesis about his psychological state.

2. **Proficient Connections:** Tesla's expert connections were additionally whimsical. He had a nearby coordinated effort with George Westinghouse, who upheld Tesla's exchanging current (AC) framework and carried it to unmistakable quality. Nonetheless, Tesla's emphasis on chasing after aggressive and frequently monetarily dangerous ventures, for example, the Wardenclyffe Pinnacle, stressed his relationship with Westinghouse and expected financial backers.

3. **Monetary Battles:** Tesla's extraordinary spotlight on his work, joined with his hesitance to popularize his developments, left him in critical monetary waterways. He frequently needed to depend on the liberality of companions and financial backers, and on occasion, he lived in devastated conditions. Tesla's monetary battles were a steady wellspring of stress and uneasiness all through his life.

4. **Over the top Impulses:** Tesla was known for his whimsies and fanatical urgent ways of behaving. He had major areas of strength for a to microbes and would frequently take part in uncommon customs to keep up with neatness. These ways of behaving additionally secluded him from social associations and added to his whimsical public picture.

Differentiating Ways to deal with Development and Connections

Edison and Tesla's varying ways to deal with advancement and connections mirror their differentiating characters and values.

Edison was a logical designer who had confidence in persevering trial and error and development. He utilized his connections and initiative abilities to collect groups of capable people and drive advancement forward. His own battles, like his hearing misfortune and conjugal hardships, were many times eclipsed by his obligation to his work and his capacity to adjust to evolving conditions.

Tesla, then again, was a visionary who focused on the quest for logical information regardless of anything else. His absence of individual connections and monetary precariousness were, to some degree, a consequence of his unfaltering devotion to his logical goals. Tesla's battles were many times self inflicted, as he would not think twice about standards or market his creations for individual addition.

The two creators confronted critical difficulties all through their lives, yet their extraordinary characters and ways to deal with development prompted particular results. Edison's sober mindedness and eagerness to adjust permitted him to make business progress and leave an enduring heritage in the realm of innovation. Tesla's constant quest for logical information and refusal to think twice about standards procured him acknowledgment as a visionary designer, despite the fact that he confronted individual and monetary difficulties.

Heritage and Illustrations

The existences of Edison and Tesla act as a wake up call of the diverse idea of virtuoso and the perplexing transaction between private connections, battles, and individual difficulties. Their varying ways to deal with development and connections exhibit that there is nobody size-fits-all recipe for progress. Edison's capacity to explore the difficulties of individual and expert life while keeping up with his productive result offers significant examples in tirelessness and versatility. On the other hand, Tesla's firm devotion to his logical beliefs highlights the significance of remaining consistent with one's standards, even notwith-standing affliction.

7.3 How their personalities influenced their inventions and business endeavors.

The characters of creators frequently assume a huge part in forming their manifestations and business pursuits. Thomas Edison and Nikola Tesla, two of the most famous creators ever, had notably various characters that significantly impacted their innovations and business attempts. In this paper, we will investigate how the

differentiating characters of Edison and Tesla formed their advancements and ways to deal with the commercialization of their developments.

Thomas Edison: The Even minded Designer and Business visionary

Thomas Edison's character was portrayed by realism, steady assurance, and a sharp innovative soul. These characteristics significantly affected his creations and business attempts.

1. **Constant Assurance:** Edison's axiom, "Virtuoso is 1% motivation and close to 100% sweat," embodies his character quality of persistent assurance. He was known for his unflinching obligation to tackling issues and conquering hindrances through sheer constancy. This assurance powered his tenacious quest for advancement.

2. **Sober mindedness:** Edison was a down to earth scholar who trusted in imagining arrangements that could be applied to day to day existence. His developments, like the phonograph, the electric light, and movies, were planned in view of reasonableness and business applications. Edison's sober minded approach guaranteed that his creations had quick and inescapable significance.

3. **Innovative Soul:** Edison had serious areas of strength for a soul. He perceived the significance of commercializing his developments and building fruitful organizations around them. In 1876, he established Menlo Park, an examination research facility

that turned into a center point for development. Afterward, he helped to establish General Electric (GE), an organization that turned into a central part in the electrical business. Edison's business astuteness permitted him to benefit from his creations and accumulate huge abundance.

4. **Cooperation and Coordinated effort:** Edison's character likewise appeared in his capacity to gather gifted groups and cultivate joint effort. He encircled himself with talented designers and creators, for example, Charles Batchelor and Francis Upton, who added to his various licenses and developments. Edison's co-operative methodology permitted him to use the aggregate skill of his group.

5. **Versatility:** Edison's character qualities of flexibility and strength were obvious in his readiness to turn and embrace new difficulties. When confronted with the ascent of rotating flow (AC) electrical frameworks supported by Nikola Tesla and George Westinghouse, Edison adjusted by further developing his own DC electrical frameworks and tracking down new applications for them.

Edison's, not entirely set in stone, and pioneering character assumed a urgent part in forming his developments and business tries. His developments tended to viable necessities and were intended for business achievement, and his capacity to fabricate powerful groups and adjust to changing conditions added to his enduring inheritance.

Nikola Tesla: The Visionary and Offbeat Virtuoso

Nikola Tesla had a character that was especially not quite the same as Edison's. He was a visionary and an offbeat virtuoso whose character impacted his extraordinary innovations and flighty way to deal with business.

1. **Visionary Reasoning:** Tesla's character was set apart by visionary reasoning. He had a profound comprehension of hypothetical

physical science and a momentous capacity to envision complex ideas. This visionary reasoning prompted a portion of his most notable innovations, like the substituting flow (AC) electrical framework and the Tesla loop. Tesla's innovations frequently pushed the limits of ordinary logical comprehension.

2. **Autonomy and Isolation:** Tesla was known for his antisocial nature and his inclination for working alone. His contemplative character drove him to focus on his logical interests over private connections and social associations. Tesla's autonomy permitted him to zero in strongly on his work, yet it additionally disengaged him from likely associates and financial backers.

3. **Whimsical Thoughts:** Tesla's capricious character reached out to his thoughts and developments. He sought after projects that were frequently forward thinking and capricious by contemporary norms. The Wardenclyffe Pinnacle, for instance, was a remote energy transmission project that was visionary at the end of the day relatively radical, prompting monetary challenges and the undertaking's relinquishment.

4. **Protection from Commercialization:** Dissimilar to Edison, Tesla was not roused by monetary profit or business achievement. His developments were driven by a craving to progress logical information and advantage mankind. This protection from commercialization frequently blocked Tesla's capacity to profit by his creations, leaving him monetarily tricky.

5. **Enthusiasm and Optimism:** Tesla's character was set apart by a profound energy for his work and a hopeful confidence in the force of science and innovation to work on the world. His obligation to his standards and goals was steadfast, even notwithstanding monetary difficulty and a disregard for one's own needs.

Tesla's visionary and unusual character affected his innovations and business attempts. His capacity to think past the bounds of the standard way of thinking prompted momentous advancements, however it additionally made it trying for him to explore the down to earth real factors of commercialization and business.

Differentiating Ways to deal with Creations and Business Development Concentration:

Edison: Edison's even minded character prompted innovations that tended to reasonable requirements and could be promptly popularized. His developments, like the electric light and phonograph, had quick applications in daily existence.

Tesla: Tesla's visionary character frequently brought about developments that were more unique and hypothetical. His emphasis was on progressing logical information, which now and again made it trying to track down quick business applications for his manifestations.

Commercialization Technique:

Edison: Edison was a wise business visionary who perceived the significance of commercializing his developments. He laid out organizations and associations to offer his developments for sale to the public effectively.

Tesla: Tesla opposed commercialization and frequently battled monetarily subsequently. His hopeful faith in the force of science frequently conflicted with the reasonable real factors of business.

Collaboration versus Freedom:

Edison: Edison's cooperative methodology permitted him to work actually with groups and influence the aggregate ability of his associates.

Tesla: Tesla's free and single nature made it trying for him to team up actually with others, frequently prompting disconnection in his work.

Inheritance:

Edison: Edison's creations quickly affected society, forming the advanced world. His heritage is attached to functional advancements that keep on impacting day to day existence.

Tesla: Tesla's heritage is established in visionary reasoning and hypothetical forward leaps that established the groundwork for the majority current advances, regardless of whether a portion of his thoughts were not promptly acknowledged during his lifetime.

Examples from Edison and Tesla

The lives and characters of Thomas Edison and Nikola Tesla offer significant illustrations for innovators and business people:

Versatility versus Determination: Edison's flexibility and readiness to turn in light of difficulties and changing conditions permitted him to make business progress. Tesla's constancy and faithful obligation to his beliefs, while visionary, likewise brought difficulties and monetary hardships.

Adjusting Vision and Common sense: Edison's reasonable way to deal with creation and business exhibited the significance of tracking down useful applications for imaginative thoughts. Tesla's optimism, while visionary, highlighted the difficulties of focusing on logical progression over commercialization.

Coordinated effort versus Autonomy: Edison's capacity to work together and construct powerful groups features the significance of working with others to make advancement and business progress. Tesla's autonomy and isolation, while helpful for extreme concentration, likewise highlight the worth of coordinated effort and systems administration.

Chapter 8

Legacy and Impact

The heritage and effect of authentic figures can frequently be estimated by the enduring impact they have on society, innovation, and culture. Thomas Edison and Nikola Tesla, two goliaths of development in the late nineteenth and mid twentieth hundreds of years, made permanent imprints on the world through their creations and commitments to science and designing. This article investigates the persevering through heritages and significant effects of Edison and Tesla, inspecting how their work keeps on forming our present reality.

Thomas Edison's Heritage and Effect

Thomas Edison, frequently alluded to as the "Wizard of Menlo Park," was a productive designer whose heritage keeps on shaping present day culture in various ways.

1. **Electric Lighting and the Light:**
   Edison's most popular innovation, the down to earth brilliant light, changed the manner in which individuals lived and worked. Preceding the boundless reception of electric lighting, social orders depended on gas lights and candles, which were expensive, wasteful, and presented fire risks. Edison's improvement of an

economically feasible light, protected in 1879, enlightened homes and organizations, expanding the useful hours of the day and fundamentally further developing security.

The tradition of Edison's light reaches out past its nearby effect. Today, the glowing bulb has been to a great extent supplanted by more energy-effective other options, like smaller fluorescent lights (CFLs) and light-discharging diodes (LEDs). Nonetheless, Edison's spearheading work in electric lighting established the groundwork for these ensuing advancements. Besides, his obligation to working on day to day existence through useful developments perseveres as a core value in current designing.

2. **Phonograph and Sound Recording:**

Edison's development of the phonograph in 1877 denoted a forward leap in the safeguarding and generation of sound. This innovation changed media outlets, empowering the recording and playback of music, discourse, and other sound

substance. The phonograph prepared for the improvement of current music recording, radio telecom, and the whole sound innovation area.

The effect of Edison's phonograph is clear in the present music industry, where computerized recording and streaming advances have democratized music creation and utilization. Without the underlying creation of sound recording by Edison, the direction of music and media innovation would have been immensely unique.

3. **Movies:**

Edison was instrumental in the early improvement of films. He fostered the kinetoscope, an early movie gadget, and the kineto-graph, a camera for catching moving pictures. These innovations laid the preparation for the entertainment world, molding how stories are told and pictured on screen.

Today, the entertainment world is a worldwide social and mone-tary force to be reckoned with, and Edison's spearheading work in films played a primary job in its development. The true to life narrating procedures and advances Edison spearheaded keep on affecting producers and craftsmen all over the planet.

4. **Electrical Power Circulation:**

Edison's commitments to electrical power circulation likewise left an enduring heritage. While Edison pushed for direct flow (DC) electrical frameworks, his work prepared for the turn of events and boundless reception of rotating flow (AC) electrical frameworks, supported by Nikola Tesla and George Westinghouse. AC electrical frameworks ended up being more productive for significant distance power transmission, and they are the premise of the cutting edge electrical lattice.

The tradition of Edison's electrical advancements should be visible in the solid power supply that powers homes, businesses, and innovation today. His initial analyses and work in electrical designing added to the advancement of the electrical framework that supports present day culture.

5. **Examination and Development Culture:**

Past unambiguous creations, Edison's way to deal with development and exploration left a getting through influence. He laid out the world's most memorable modern exploration lab in Menlo Park, New Jersey, in 1876. This lab turned into a model for resulting innovative work offices, including the cutting edge idea of corporate exploration labs. Edison's accentuation on trial and error, cooperation, and deliberate creation set a trend for development rehearses in different ventures.

The tradition of Edison's examination culture should be visible in the endless labs and development focuses that keep on driving mechanical progressions across different

fields. His obligation to the methodical quest for information and development stays a wellspring of motivation for researchers, specialists, and innovators.

In rundown, Thomas Edison's heritage is described by his spearheading developments, commitments to electrical designing, and getting through influence on mechanical advancement. His work in electric lighting, sound recording, films, electrical power conveyance, and exploration approach has molded current culture and keeps on impacting different areas of science and innovation.

Nikola Tesla's Heritage and Effect

Nikola Tesla, frequently viewed as an offbeat virtuoso and a visionary creator, left an exceptional and powerful heritage that has earned expanding acknowledgment as of late.

1. **Rotating Flow (AC) Electrical Frameworks:**

   One of Tesla's most huge commitments to the world was the turn of events and advancement of substituting flow (AC) electrical frameworks. Tesla's work on AC power established the groundwork for present day electrical power conveyance, empowering the productive transmission of power over significant distances. His creative work straightforwardly tested Edison's backing for direct current (DC) frameworks.

   The getting through effect of Tesla's AC electrical frameworks is clear in the present electrical network, which depends dominatingly on AC power for age, transmission, and conveyance. Tesla's vision for a worldwide electrical matrix, controlled by AC power, keeps on impacting the plan and activity of electrical frameworks around the world.

2. **Remote Correspondence and Radio:**

   Tesla's analyses with remote correspondence and radio waves fundamentally added to the advancement of radio innovation. While he frequently didn't get legitimate credit during his lifetime, Tesla's work on remote transmission of transmissions laid the preparation for current radio correspondence.

   The tradition of Tesla's work in remote correspondence is obvious in the far reaching utilization of radio, TV broadcasting, and remote advances, which have changed worldwide correspondence and amusement. His spearheading endeavors in this field keep on impacting remote innovation improvement.

3. **Tesla Loop and High-Recurrence Gadgets:**

Tesla's creation of the Tesla loop, a high-recurrence thunderous transformer, denoted a leap forward in the age of high-voltage and high-recurrence electrical flows. While at first utilized for logical examinations and exhibitions, the Tesla loop has found applications in fields like media communications, clinical gadgets, and diversion.

Tesla's commitments to high-recurrence hardware stay applicable today, especially in the improvement of advances like radio-frequency ID (RFID), remote power move, and clinical imaging. His developments in this space keep on molding present day electronic gadgets and frameworks.

4. **Remote Power Transmission:**

Tesla's visionary idea of remote power transmission, exemplified by his Wardenclyffe Pinnacle project, has enlivened continuous innovative work in the field of remote energy move. Albeit the Wardenclyffe Pinnacle project was never finished because of monetary imperatives, the possibility of remote energy transmission keeps on being investigated in different structures, including remote charging for electronic gadgets and electric vehicles.

Tesla's vision for remote power transmission stays a wellspring of motivation for scientists and trailblazers trying to saddle remote energy move for pragmatic applications, like feasible energy dispersion.

5. **Environmentally friendly power and Maintainability:**

As of late, Tesla's thoughts on environmentally friendly power and manageable advances stand out. His vision for tackling normal energy sources, for example, sun based and wind power, lines up with contemporary endeavors to progress to cleaner and more supportable energy frameworks.

Tesla's heritage in environmentally friendly power and supportability should be visible in the turn of events and reception of advances like sunlight based chargers, wind turbines, and electric vehicles. His spearheading soul in looking for imaginative answers for address natural difficulties reverberates with current worldwide endeavors to moderate environmental change.

6. Social Symbol and Motivation:

Past his logical and designing commitments, Tesla has turned into a social symbol and an image of whimsical virtuoso. His life and work have motivated various books, films, and imaginative translations. Tesla's baffling character, unconventionalities, and obligation to his goals have caught the creative mind of individuals around the world.

Tesla's persevering through influence as a social figure highlights the force of individual vision and assurance to motivate people in the future. He keeps on being an image of development and imagination even with misfortune.

Contrasting Edison and Tesla's Inheritances:

While both Edison and Tesla left striking inheritances, their methodologies and areas of impact contrast fundamentally:

Edison's inheritance is portrayed by viable innovations that straightforwardly affected day to day existence, like electric lighting and sound recording. His accentuation on commercialization and precise exploration left a significant effect on industry and development culture.

Tesla's heritage, then again, is set apart by visionary thoughts and commitments to essential advancements like AC power, radio, and remote correspondence. His work frequently centered around logical headway and hypothetical forward leaps, with applications that reached out a long ways past his lifetime.

The two designers were instrumental in forming the cutting edge world, with their developments spreading over assorted areas of science and innovation. Their heritages keep on affecting contemporary examination, advancement, and social talk.

The Convergence of Edison and Tesla's Inheritances:

Edison's spearheading work in electric lighting and power dissemination impacted the framework whereupon Tesla's AC electrical frameworks were constructed. Together, their commitments molded the cutting edge electrical matrix.

Tesla's work on radio waves and remote correspondence advances has establishes in Edison's work on sound recording and transmission. The advancement of radio and media communications drew from developments by the two innovators.

Edison's foundation of examination labs and methodical creation rehearses set a trend for logical and designing exploration, which impacted resulting ages of innovators and scientists, remembering those working for advances propelled by Tesla's thoughts.

In this sense, the traditions of Edison and Tesla are interconnected, mirroring the cooperative and aggregate nature of mechanical advancement.

Instructive and Helpful Heritages:

Edison's obligation to schooling and the spread of information is apparent in his foundation of the Edison Establishment, which later turned into The Henry Portage Exhibition hall of American Advancement. This organization keeps on motivating youthful personalities and observe American resourcefulness.

Tesla's heritage is propagated through associations like the Tesla Science Center at Wardenclyffe, committed to saving his research facility and advancing logical training. Tesla's unusual way to deal with development fills in as a motivation for imaginative masterminds and designers.

8.1 An exploration of the lasting legacies of Edison and Tesla in electrical engineering.

The universe of electrical designing has been formed by the splendid personalities and advancements of various trailblazers. Two names that reliably ascend to the front of any conversation about the historical backdrop of electrical designing are Thomas Edison and Nikola Tesla.

These two visionaries, albeit frequently viewed as adversaries, made significant and enduring commitments to the field, each making a permanent imprint on the manner in which we outfit and use power. This paper will dig into the getting through traditions of Edison and Tesla in electrical designing, analyzing their singular accomplishments, commitments, and the effect they have had on the world we live in today.

Edison's Getting through Heritage

Thomas Edison, frequently alluded to as "The Wizard of Menlo Park," was a productive creator who held more than 1,000 licenses during his lifetime. His commitments to electrical designing and innovation overall are complex, and a large number of his creations keep on impacting present day life.

The Radiant Light: Edison's most renowned creation is without a doubt the brilliant light, protected in 1879. This development altered lighting and made ready for the jolt of homes and urban communities around the world. While radiant bulbs have been generally supplanted by more energy-productive choices today, they stay an image of Edison's resourcefulness and vision.

The Electrical Power Framework: Edison's work stretched out past the light. He fostered the primary functional electrical power age and dispersion framework, known as immediate flow (DC). Edison's DC framework assumed a pivotal part in charging metropolitan regions during the late nineteenth 100 years. While it has to a great extent been supplanted by rotating flow (AC) frameworks, his commitments to electrical framework were essential.

Sound Recording: Edison was likewise a trailblazer in sound innovation. He developed the phonograph, the primary gadget fit for both recording and repeating sound. This

advancement laid the preparation for the music and media outlet, impacting the improvement of present day recording and playback gadgets.

The Movie Camera: Edison's kinetoscope and kinetograph innovations were among the earliest movie cameras, adding to the introduction of the entertainment world. His work in this space helped shape the universe of diversion and visual narrating.

The Innovative work Model: Past his singular creations, Edison's way to deal with innovative work left an enduring heritage. He laid out the world's most memorable modern exploration research facility in Menlo Park, New Jersey, where he and his group led broad trials and fostered various developments. This model of coordinated, efficient exploration and advancement established the groundwork for present day innovative work rehearses.

Tesla's Getting through Heritage

Nikola Tesla, a Serbian-American creator and designer, is many times depicted as Edison's opponent, however their ways to deal with electrical designing varied essentially. Tesla's commitments to the field were similarly earth shattering, and his thoughts keep on molding our advanced world.

Rotating Flow (AC): Tesla's most critical commitment was the turn of events and advancement of AC electrical frameworks. He showed the predominance of AC over DC in sending power over significant distances proficiently. Today, AC power dissemination is the worldwide norm, thanks to a great extent to Tesla's work. His developments, for example, the air conditioner acceptance engine and transformer, stay fundamental parts of electrical lattices around the world.

Remote Power Transmission: Tesla's visionary thoughts reached out past wired electrical frameworks. He imagined a reality where power could be sent remotely, and in spite of the fact that his remote power transmission tests confronted difficulties, his thoughts prepared for current remote advancements and the chance of remote charging.

Radio Innovation: Tesla's work on radio innovation was central for the improvement of remote correspondence. While Guglielmo Marconi is frequently credited with creating the radio, Tesla's earlier work on radio waves and transmitters laid the basis for this progressive innovation.

Tesla Loop: The Tesla curl, an electrical full transformer circuit, was imagined by Nikola Tesla in the late nineteenth 100 years. While it at first had restricted functional applications, it has turned into an image of logical trial and error and keeps on enrapturing devotees and scientists today.

Controller and Advanced mechanics: Tesla additionally spearheaded controller innovation and imagined the improvement of advanced mechanics. His creations in this

space foreshadowed the advancement of present day robotization and controller frameworks.

Looking at Their Heritages

Edison and Tesla were the two goliaths in the field of electrical designing, however their methodologies and commitments contrasted essentially. Edison was a reasonable creator who zeroed in on commercializing and adapting his developments. His work significantly affected the regular routines of individuals, from giving light to empowering sound recording and films.

Tesla, then again, was a visionary scholar and creator who frequently focused on logical revelation over business achievement. His advancements established the groundwork for the vast majority of the innovations we depend on today, including AC power circulation and remote correspondence. While he battled monetarily during his lifetime, his thoughts lastingly affect the world.

It's essential to take note of that Edison and Tesla's competition is much of the time exaggerated in mainstream society. While they had various methodologies and in some cases clashing perspectives on electrical frameworks, they additionally had common regard for one another's work. Edison perceived the significance of Tesla's AC framework, and Tesla respected Edison's useful creations.

Their heritages in electrical designing are corresponding as opposed to problematic. Edison's emphasis on useful applications and foundation advancement carried power to homes and urban communities, while Tesla's developments in electrical hypothesis and remote advances extended the conceivable outcomes of electrical designing.

Current Utilizations of Edison and Tesla's Work

The traditions of Edison and Tesla keep on molding the field of electrical designing and straightforwardly affect our lives today.

Electrical Power Conveyance: Tesla's AC power dispersion framework stays the norm for sending power across immense distances. This framework is the foundation of

present day electrical networks, guaranteeing that power can be created at far off areas and disseminated productively to homes, organizations, and ventures.

Lighting: Albeit brilliant bulbs are less regularly utilized because of their failure, Edison's work on lighting innovation prepared for the improvement of current lighting arrangements, including minimized fluorescent lights (CFLs), light-emanating diodes (LEDs), and shrewd lighting frameworks.

Electrical Engines: Tesla's AC enlistment engine is broadly utilized in different applications, from modern apparatus to home devices. Its effectiveness and unwavering quality make it a foundation of electrical designing.

Remote Correspondence: Tesla's commitments to radio innovation were instrumental in the advancement of current remote correspondence frameworks, including radio telecom, cell organizations, and Wi-Fi.

Controller and Mechanization: Tesla's work on controller established the groundwork for the advancement of remote-controlled gadgets, robotized frameworks, and mechanical technology. Today, we see the impact of his thoughts in enterprises going from assembling to medical services.

Remote Charging: Tesla's vision of remote power transmission has seen reestablished interest lately, especially in the improvement of remote charging advancements for electronic gadgets and electric vehicles.

8.2 How their innovations continue to shape our modern world.

The traditions of Thomas Edison and Nikola Tesla in the field of electrical designing are not bound to history books or historical centers. Their spearheading developments proceed to shape and impact our advanced world in significant ways. From the manner in which we create and convey power to the advances we depend on for correspondence, transportation, and day to day existence, Edison and Tesla's commitments are woven into the texture of our reality. This exposition investigates what their advancements relentlessly mean for our contemporary society.

Edison's Getting through Impact

The Glowing Light: Edison's most notorious creation, the radiant light, may have advanced into more energy-proficient choices like Drove bulbs, yet its key rule of changing over electrical energy into light actually supports current lighting innovation. The idea of brightening without an open fire upset homes, urban communities, and

ventures, and the present lighting advances owe their reality to Edison's spearheading work.

Electrical Power Appropriation: While Edison supported direct flow (DC) for electrical power dissemination, it was Tesla's substituting flow (AC) framework that eventually won. Notwithstanding, Edison's commitments to early electrical foundation laid the preparation for the broad electrical networks that power our homes and enterprises today. His attention on reasonableness security principles actually illuminate the plan and guideline regarding electrical frameworks.

Sound Recording and Diversion: Edison's creation of the phonograph changed the manner in which we catch and duplicate sound. From vinyl records to computerized streaming, the standards of sound recording and playback he spearheaded keep on being at the core of the music and media outlet. His development empowered the conservation of music, discourse, and other hear-able encounters, forming our social legacy.

Movies and Visual Narrating: Edison's kinetoscope and kinetograph assumed crucial parts in the advancement of films. Today, the entertainment world stands as a demonstration of the force of visual narrating, a work of art that has extended from quiet movies to cutting edge computerized film. Edison's commitments to this field keep on spellbinding crowds around the world.

Innovative work Practices: Edison's foundation of the primary modern examination lab in Menlo Park, New Jersey, established the groundwork for current innovative work (Research and development) rehearses. The precise way to deal with development, trial and error, and cooperation he acquainted go on with be a foundation of Research and development in different enterprises, from innovation to drugs.

Tesla's Enduring Effect

Substituting Flow (AC) Power Dispersion: Tesla's promotion for AC electrical frameworks reformed how power is communicated and circulated. His AC engine and transformer plans empowered proficient significant distance power transmission, making it conceivable to produce power at far off areas and supply it to urban communities and businesses. The Air conditioner framework stays the foundation of current electrical networks around the world.

Remote Correspondence: Tesla's work on radio waves and transmitters established the groundwork for remote correspondence innovations. His commitments made ready

for radio telecom, cell organizations, satellite correspondence, and Wi-Fi, empowering worldwide availability and data trade. Today, we convey the tradition of his thoughts in our cell phones, PCs, and IoT gadgets.

Remote Power Transmission: Despite the fact that Tesla's fantasy of remote power transmission has not yet been completely understood, his trials and ideas have prodded interest in remote charging advancements. Electric vehicles (EVs) and electronic gadgets progressively utilize remote charging, decreasing the dependence on actual connectors and lines.

Controller and Robotization: Tesla's imaginative work on controller innovation and the advancement of remote-controlled gadgets laid the foundation for present day computerization and mechanical technology. His vision of machines equipped for independent activity finds articulation in businesses going from assembling and medical services to space investigation.

Tesla Curls and Logical Trial and error: While Tesla loops might have restricted pragmatic applications, they represent Tesla's obligation to logical investigation and interest driven research. His unpredictable way to deal with understanding power and energy keeps on moving researchers and creators to push the limits of what is conceivable.

Looking at Their Getting through Impact

Edison and Tesla's developments, while unmistakable in numerous ways, have met to shape the cutting edge world. Their heritages keep on affecting different parts of our lives, from how we enlighten our homes to how we impart, travel, and tackle energy.

Practical Energy: Both Edison and Tesla assumed parts in the improvement of electrical power frameworks, yet with contrasting methodologies. While Edison zeroed in on DC frameworks, Tesla's AC framework won the fight for productivity in significant distance power transmission. Today, this air conditioner framework is the reason for environmentally friendly power age and circulation, as it permits us to move power from distant sustainable sources, like breeze and sun based ranches, to where it is required most.

Electric Transportation: Tesla's work on electrical power and engines has tracked down recharged significance in the time of electric vehicles (EVs). The Air conditioner enlistment engine he spearheaded is a crucial part of current EVs, adding to their

proficiency and execution. Edison's work on batteries and energy stockpiling additionally laid the foundation for current electric vehicle innovation.

Remote Innovation: Edison's commitments to sound recording and playback, alongside Tesla's work on radio waves, have converged to make the remote sound innovation we depend on today, from Bluetooth speakers to remote earphones. This consistent network has turned into a vital piece of our day to day routines.

Robotization and Advanced mechanics: Tesla's interest with controller and computerization is reflected in the improvement of independent robots, robots, and

self-driving vehicles. Edison's obligation to precise examination rehearses has likewise impacted the improvement of man-made consciousness and AI, which are essential to current mechanization.

Correspondence and Network: The cooperative energy among Edison and Tesla's work in electrical designing supports our cutting edge correspondence frameworks. Edison's advancements in sound innovation, joined with Tesla's commitments to remote correspondence, have prompted the improvement of gadgets that permit us to convey and get to data momentarily from anyplace on the planet.

Logical Revelation: Tesla's strange trials and hunger for logical information keep on moving people in the future of researchers and creators. His soul of interest and investigation urges scientists to push the limits of what is known and to look for unpredictable answers for complex issues.

Challenges and Moral Contemplations

While Edison and Tesla's developments have irrefutably formed our cutting edge world, their heritages additionally raise significant difficulties and moral contemplations.

Supportability: The fast development in power interest, mostly determined by the advances Edison and Tesla spearheaded, has raised worries about manageability and ecological effect. Tending to these difficulties requires a shift toward environmentally friendly power sources, energy proficiency, and mindful utilization.

Admittance to Innovation: The advantages of Edison and Tesla's advancements are not similarly circulated around the world. Admittance to present day electrical framework, correspondence organizations, and trend setting innovations stays inconsistent, adding to the computerized partition. Overcoming this issue is significant for accomplishing worldwide value and success.

Protection and Security: The interconnectedness of our cutting edge world, driven to some degree by remote correspondence and computerization, presents new difficulties connected with security and network safety. Guaranteeing the security of individual information and basic framework while keeping up with individual protection privileges is a continuous concern.

Innovative Joblessness: Computerization and mechanical technology, affected by the dreams of Edison and Tesla, can possibly uproot customary positions. Society should address the difficulties of mechanical joblessness by putting resources into instruction

and preparing projects to furnish the labor force with the abilities required for the positions representing things to come.

8.3 The broader implications of their rivalry for technological progress.

The competition between Thomas Edison and Nikola Tesla is quite possibly of the most notorious and frequently romanticized fight throughout the entire existence of science and innovation. These two splendid personalities, with their contrasting ways to deal with electrical designing, were innovators as well as visionaries who molded the course of mechanical advancement. Their contention had sweeping ramifications that drawn out quite a ways past their lifetimes and keep on impacting the direction of development and innovative turn of events. In this paper, we will investigate the more extensive ramifications of their competition for mechanical advancement, zeroing in on its effect on research culture, protected innovation, development, and the improvement of electrical framework.

Research Culture and Cooperation versus Rivalry:

Edison: Edison's way to deal with development was portrayed by contest and the security of protected innovation. He had faith in the worth of individual exertion and kept a climate of mystery in his Menlo Park research facility. Edison's techniques were driven by commercialization and the need to produce benefits from his developments. While this approach prompted fast turn of events and protecting of various functional gadgets, it additionally prevented the spread of information and cooperative examination.

Tesla: conversely, Tesla's methodology was more open and cooperative. He was driven by a longing to progress logical information and trusted in the free trade of thoughts. Tesla frequently battled monetarily because of his absence of spotlight on commercialization and licensing, yet his readiness to share thoughts and team up with different researchers and designers added to the more extensive academic local area's development.

Suggestion: The competition among Edison and Tesla mirrors the pressure between exclusive advancement and open coordinated effort in mechanical advancement. While rivalry can drive quick headways and the commercialization of innovations, it might likewise restrict the sharing of information and cooperative leap forwards. The harmony among rivalry and joint effort keeps on being a subject of discussion in contemporary exploration culture.

Licensed innovation and Advancement:

Edison: Edison was a productive innovator who held more than 1,000 licenses during his lifetime. He figured out the significance of safeguarding licensed innovation through licenses and laid out a model for patent-based development. His emphasis on getting licenses permitted him to fabricate a fruitful business realm around his creations, like the electric light.

Tesla: Tesla held various licenses also, yet his way to deal with protected innovation was less business driven. He frequently focused on logical revelation over monetary benefit and didn't completely take advantage of the business capability of a portion of his creations, like remote power transmission. This approach prompted monetary battles yet left a tradition of thoughts and innovations that impacted later creators.

Suggestion: The contention among Edison and Tesla features the strain between patent-driven development and the quest for logical information for the good of its own. Today, this strain stays pertinent as organizations wrestle with how to adjust safeguarding their developments through licenses while adding to open-source and cooperative advancement endeavors.

Advancement and Foundation Improvement:

Edison: Edison's advancements frequently centered around commonsense applications and foundation improvement. His work on the electrical power framework, including the improvement of the immediate flow (DC) framework, assumed a vital part in carrying power to metropolitan regions and driving homes and enterprises. His accentuation on framework made electrical frameworks open to the majority.

Tesla: Tesla's developments, like the substituting flow (AC) power framework, zeroed in on working on the productivity and significant distance transmission of power. His work established the groundwork for the cutting edge electrical framework, which empowers power age at far off areas and effective conveyance to urban communities and enterprises.

Suggestion: The competition among Edison and Tesla exhibited the significance of both reasonable, foundation arranged development and undeniable level hypothetical progressions. This duality keeps on impacting mechanical advancement today, as we balance the requirement for sure fire down to earth arrangements with long haul, groundbreaking developments.

Public Discernment and Well known Science:

Edison: Edison was an expert of advertising and figured out the benefit of showcasing his innovations. He frequently got significant media inclusion and turned into a commonly recognized name. This public acknowledgment supported his standing as well as made energy and interest in mechanical advancement.

Tesla: Tesla, in spite of his critical commitments, didn't partake in similar degree of public acknowledgment during his lifetime. His work on remote correspondence and transmission of power, while pivotal, was less open to the overall population. It was exclusively in later years that Tesla's commitments got the acknowledgment they merited.

Suggestion: The competition among Edison and Tesla highlights the job of public discernment and well known science in molding the course of mechanical advancement. The public's interest with creators and their developments can impact subsidizing, backing, and public approaches connected with science and innovation.

Heritage and Motivation:

Edison: Edison's inheritance is frequently connected with useful developments that straightforwardly affect day to day existence. His commitments to lighting, sound recording, and films stay notorious and powerful. His way to deal with development, stressing commercialization and substantial items, has made an enduring imprint on the field.

Tesla: Tesla's heritage is portrayed by visionary thoughts and weighty ideas that reached out past the functional uses of his time. His work on AC power transmission, remote correspondence, and controller keeps on moving innovators and researchers. While his creations might have been less promptly popularized, they have impacted later advancements in innovation.

Suggestion: The competition among Edison and Tesla shows how various ways to deal with development can prompt changing heritages. Reasonable designers like Edison leave a tradition of substantial items, while visionaries like Tesla leave a tradition of thoughts and ideas that keep on driving development and logical interest.

Chapter 9

Beyond Edison and Tesla

The traditions of Thomas Edison and Nikola Tesla in the areas of science and innovation are unquestionably significant, however the scene of advancement is immense and populated by various other powerful figures. These people have made huge commitments to assorted areas, from material science and arithmetic to science, registering, and space investigation. This exposition leaves on an extensive excursion to investigate the lives, works, and persevering through effects of a portion of these extraordinary figures past Edison and Tesla. By digging into their accounts, we gain bits of knowledge into the multifaceted snare of progress that has molded our cutting edge world.

1. **Marie Curie: A Trailblazer in Radioactivity and Radiation Treatment**

   Marie Curie, a Clean conceived physicist and scientist, was a pioneer in the field of radioactivity. She was the main lady to win a Nobel Prize and stays the main individual to have gotten Nobel Prizes in two different logical fields (Physical science in 1903 and Science in 1911). Curie's weighty examination on radioactivity prompted the disclosure of radium and polonium, and she created strategies to disengage radioactive isotopes.

Her work established the groundwork for current atomic material science and science.

One of the main traditions of Marie Curie is her spearheading commitments to the field of clinical science. She perceived the capability of radioactive materials in treating disease, and her exploration prepared for radiation treatment. Today, radiation treatment is a basic device in the battle against disease, saving endless lives.

2. **Alan Turing: The Dad of Software engineering**

Alan Turing, an English mathematician, rationalist, and PC researcher, is in many cases viewed as the dad of software engineering. His notable work during the twentieth century established the hypothetical starting point for current PCs and computerized reasoning. Turing's conceptualization of the "Turing machine," a hypothetical computational gadget, assumed an essential part in characterizing the limits of what can be processed algorithmically. During The Second Great War, Turing's work at Bletchley Park was instrumental in breaking the German Riddle code, an accomplishment that essentially added to the Partnered triumph. His commitments to cryptography, as well as his hypothetical experiences into calculation, keep on molding the fields of network safety, software engineering, and computer based intelligence today.

3. **Rosalind Franklin: Divulging the Construction of DNA**

Rosalind Franklin, an English scientist and crystallographer, made basic commitments to the comprehension of DNA's construction. Her X-beam diffraction investigations of DNA filaments gave essential information that were instrumental in the revelation of the DNA twofold helix structure by James Watson and Francis Cramp in 1953. While Franklin's work was critical, she frequently didn't get the acknowledgment she merited during her lifetime.

Today, how we might interpret hereditary qualities and the underpinning of biotechnology and genomics is well established in the revelation of the DNA structure. Rosalind Franklin's commitments to this revelation act as a wake up call of the significance of perceiving crafted by researchers who might not have accepted their due acknowledgment in their time.

4. **Albert Einstein: The Hypothesis of Relativity and the Cutting edge Comprehension of the Universe**

Albert Einstein, a German-conceived physicist, is eminent for his momentous hypotheses of relativity. His extraordinary hypothesis of relativity, distributed in 1905, presented the idea of space-time and re-imagined how we might interpret existence. His popular condition, E=mc^2, exhibited the proportionality of mass and energy, prompting headways in atomic material science and the advancement of thermal power.

Einstein's overall hypothesis of relativity, distributed in 1915, presented the idea of gravity as the twisting of spacetime. This hypothesis has had significant ramifications for how we might interpret the universe, including the expectation and ensuing affirmation of peculiarities like gravitational lensing and the presence of dark openings.

The tradition of Albert Einstein stretches out a long ways past hypothetical material science. His work established the groundwork for various mechanical advancements, including the improvement of GPS, as his speculations represent the relativistic impacts of satellite movement.

5. **Ada Lovelace: The World's Most memorable Software engineer**

Ada Lovelace, an English mathematician and essayist, is commended as the world's most memorable software engineer. During the nineteenth 100 years, Lovelace worked close by Charles Babbage, a trailblazer of mechanical processing gadgets known as "scientific motors."

Lovelace's surprising experiences incorporated the acknowledgment that these machines could be customized to play out a large number of undertakings past simple mathematical computations.

Her earth shattering notes on Babbage's work, especially her itemized directions for how to program the insightful motor to ascertain Bernoulli numbers, mark the introduction of PC programming. Lovelace's visionary thoughts laid the preparation for the improvement of present day programming dialects and programming.

The customs of Thomas Edison and Nikola Tesla in the space of science and development are verifiably critical, but the location of progression is gigantic and populated by different other strong figures. These individuals have committed to arranged regions, from material science and number juggling to science, enlisting, and space examination. This composition passes on a broad journey to examine the lives, works, and persisting through impacts of a part of these remarkable figures past Edison and Tesla. By diving into their records, we gain pieces of information into the multi-layered catch of progress that has formed our state of the art world.

1. **Marie Curie: A Pioneer in Radioactivity and Radiation Therapy**

   Marie Curie, a Clean imagined physicist and researcher, was a trailblazer in the field ofradioactivity. She was the primary woman to win a Nobel Prize and stays the principal individual to have gotten Nobel Prizes in two different legitimate fields (Actual science in 1903 and Science in 1911). Curie's significant assessment on radioactivity provoked the divulgence of radium and polonium, and she thought up procedures to withdraw radioactive isotopes. Her work laid out the foundation for current nuclear material science and science.

   One of the primary customs of Marie Curie is her leading responsibilities to the field of clinical science. She saw the ability of radioactive materials in treating illness, and her investigation arranged for radiation therapy. Today, radiation therapy is an essential gadget in the fight against sickness, saving vast lives.

2. **Alan Turing: The Father of Programming**

Alan Turing, an English mathematician, realist, and PC scientist, is generally speaking seen as the father of programming. His prominent work during the 20th century laid out the speculative beginning stage for current laptops and electronic thinking. Turing's conceptualization of the "Turing machine," a speculative computational contraption,

expected a fundamental part in describing the constraints of what can be handled algorithmically.

During The Subsequent Extraordinary Conflict, Turing's work at Bletchley Park was instrumental in breaking the German Enigma code, an achievement that basically added to the Cooperated win. His responsibilities to cryptography, as well as his speculative encounters into estimation, continue to form the fields of organization security, programming, and PC based insight today.

3. **Rosalind Franklin: Unveiling the Development of DNA**

Rosalind Franklin, an English researcher and crystallographer, committed to the understanding of DNA's development. Her X-bar diffraction examinations of DNA fibers gave fundamental data that were instrumental in the disclosure of the DNA twofold helix structure by James Watson and Francis Spasm in 1953. While Franklin's work was basic, she every now and again didn't get the affirmation she justified during her lifetime.

Today, how we could decipher genetic characteristics and the supporting of biotechnology and genomics is deep rooted in the disclosure of the DNA structure. Rosalind Franklin's responsibilities to this disclosure go about as a reminder of the meaning of seeing created by specialists who probably won't have acknowledged their due affirmation in their time.

4. **Albert Einstein: The Speculation of Relativity and the State of the art Appreciation of the Universe**

Albert Einstein, a German-imagined physicist, is prominent for his groundbreaking theories of relativity. His phenomenal speculation of relativity, dispersed in 1905, introduced the possibility of spacetime and rethought how we could decipher presence. His well known condition, E=mc^2, showed the proportionality of mass and energy, provoking types of progress in nuclear material science and the headway of nuclear energy.

Einstein's general speculation of relativity, appropriated in 1915, introduced the possibility of gravity as the bending of spacetime. This speculation has had huge implications for how we could decipher the universe, including the assumption and resulting insistence of quirks like gravitational lensing and the presence of dim openings.

The custom of Albert Einstein loosens up far past speculative material science. His work laid out the preparation for different mechanical progressions, including the improvement of GPS, as his hypotheses address the relativistic effects of satellite development.

5. Ada Lovelace: The World's Most vital Programmer

Ada Lovelace, an English mathematician and writer, is recognized as the world's most critical computer programmer. During the nineteenth 100 years, Lovelace worked nearby Charles Babbage, a pioneer of mechanical handling devices known as "logical engines." Lovelace's amazing encounters consolidated the affirmation that these machines could be tweaked to play out countless endeavors past straightforward numerical calculations.

Her momentous notes on Babbage's work, particularly her organized bearings for how to program the wise engine to learn Bernoulli numbers, mark the presentation of PC programming. Lovelace's visionary contemplations laid the groundwork to improve present day programming lingos and programming.

9.1A look at the subsequent developments in electrical engineering and technology.

The field of electrical planning and advancement has gone through striking movements since the leading work of figures like Thomas Edison and Nikola Tesla. The focal disclosures and improvements of these early lights laid the groundwork for an exceptional trip that continues to shape our state of the art world. In this work, we will research the subsequent upgrades in electrical planning and development, following the improvement of key advances, the ascent of new norms, and the impact on various pieces of our lives.

1. **The Rising of Subbing Current (AC) Power Systems:**

   While Thomas Edison upheld direct stream (DC) for electrical power transport, it was Nikola Tesla's pivoting stream (AC) system that finally won. The new development and wide gathering of AC power structures changed the age, transport, and utilization of force.

   The change to AC power brought different benefits, including the ability to send control over huge distances capably. This laid out the basis for the state of the art electrical grid, which enables power age at distant regions and the assignment of capacity to homes, associations, and organizations.

   Today, AC power remains the overall standard for electrical systems, supporting the strong reserve of ability to control our homes, mechanical assemblies, and present day equipment. The capable transmission of AC power has also made it possible to saddle energy from limitless sources like breeze and sun situated farms, adding to the improvement of legitimate energy game plans.

2. **Shock of Transportation:**

   One of the basic headways in electrical planning and advancement is the charge of transportation. The advancement from internal combustion engines to electric vehicles (EVs) has gotten a move on lately, with electric vehicles, transports, and even trucks ending up being dynamically ordinary on roads all over the planet.

The development of EVs is driven by types of progress in battery advancement, including the improvement of lithium-molecule batteries with higher energy thickness and longer futures. These batteries are controlling explorer vehicles as well as electric endlessly bicycles, offering cleaner and more capable transportation decisions.

The shock of transportation contacts public travel structures and the flying business, where electric and cross variety electric plane are being made. These improvements intend to decrease ozone draining substance releases, decline dependence on non-sustainable power sources, and add to a more commonsense future.

3. **Harmless to the ecosystem power Mix:**
   The compromise of supportable power sources, similar to breeze, sun situated, and hydroelectric power, into the electrical structure has changed the energy scene. Advances in electrical planning play had a critical effect in outfitting and capably coursing energy from these sources.

   Canny system advancements, for instance, engage consistent checking and control of force movement, propelling the use of harmless to the ecosystem power and further creating network strength. Battery energy limit structures have moreover emerged as crucial parts, allowing excess energy from renewables to be taken care of and dispatched when required.

   Microgrids, which are confined energy systems that can work independently or connected with the essential grid, are ending up being dynamically inescapable. They give adaptability during system interferences and work with the fuse of coursed energy resources, including daylight fueled chargers and little wind turbines, at the neighborhood.

The drive toward a more practical energy mix, constrained by renewables, mirrors the creating cognizance of regular concerns and the need to ease natural change. It is an exhibition of the gig of electrical planning in shaping a greener and more efficient future.

4. **Significant level Correspondence Headways:**

The field of correspondence development has seen a quick turn of events, driven by headways in electrical planning and information development. The progression of high

speed data transmission and far off correspondence developments has changed how we partner, grant, and access information.

The rollout of 4G and 5G associations has presented a time of ubiquitous accessibility, enabling speedier web access, low-lethargy correspondence, and the increase of IoT (Web of Things) devices. These headways have ideas for various regions, including clinical benefits, transportation, and splendid metropolitan networks.

Fiber-optic correspondence structures, another accomplishment in electrical planning, have enabled the transmission of gigantic proportions of data over huge distances with immaterial sign setback. This advancement shapes the groundwork of high speed web affiliations and supports numerous applications, from video constant to telemedicine.

The change to decentralized energy age, where individual purchasers can make and store their own power, is reshaping the customary utility model. Microgrids, referred to earlier, are a sign of this example, enabling restricted energy age and usage.

6. **Economical and Proficient Structure Innovations:**

Progressions in electrical designing have added to the improvement of economical and energy-effective structure advances. Shrewd structures, furnished with sensors, robotization frameworks, and energy the executives arrangements, advance energy utilization, further develop solace, and lessen natural effect.

Energy-productive lighting frameworks, like Drove lighting, have turned into the norm, offering huge energy investment funds contrasted with conventional radiant and glaring lights. These frameworks are constrained by cutting edge lighting the board frameworks that adjust to normal lighting conditions and inhabitance.

Environmentally friendly power coordination in structures, including sunlight based chargers and little wind turbines, has become progressively normal, considering nearby power age and decreased dependence on the network. Energy-productive central air (warming, ventilation, and cooling) frameworks further improve building manageability.

7. Mechanical technology and Computerization:

The field of advanced mechanics and mechanization has been extraordinarily impacted by electrical designing and innovation. Modern robots have become vital to assembling processes, performing undertakings with accuracy and effectiveness. Cooperative robots, or cobots, are intended to work close by people, improving efficiency and wellbeing in different businesses.

Notwithstanding modern applications, mechanical technology and computerization have tracked down their direction into medical care, coordinated factors, horticulture, and even space investigation. Careful robots help specialists in carrying out complex

systems with more noteworthy accuracy, while independent vehicles and robots are altering transportation and operations.

8. Space Investigation and Satellite Innovation:

Electrical designing plays had a critical impact in propelling space investigation and satellite innovation. The advancement of space apparatus, correspondence satellites, and logical instruments has extended how we might interpret the universe and worked with worldwide availability.

Progressions in scaling down and power proficiency have prompted the arrangement of more modest, practical satellites known as Cube-Sats. These satellites are utilized for different purposes, including Earth perception, logical exploration, and media communications.

Besides, the investigation of Mars, the Moon, and other heavenly bodies has been made conceivable through electrical designing advancements. Wanderers, landers, and space apparatus furnished with complex instrumentation have given significant experiences into planetary topography and the potential for extraterrestrial life.

9. Biomedical Designing and Medical care Innovation:

The crossing point of electrical designing and biomedical science has led to notable medical services advancements. Clinical imaging gadgets, like X-ray (attractive reverberation imaging) and CT (registered tomography) scanners, depend on cutting edge hardware and sign handling strategies to give itemized indicative data.

Electrocardiography (ECG or EKG) and electroencephalography (EEG) are demonstrative procedures that record electrical movement in the heart and cerebrum, separately. These advancements help in the analysis and observing of cardiovascular and neurological circumstances.

Implantable clinical gadgets, for example, pacemakers and cochlear inserts, influence electrical designing standards to reestablish and improve physiological capabilities. Moreover, wearable wellbeing observing gadgets, like wellness trackers and smartwatches, have become vital to individual wellbeing the board.

10. Environmentally friendly power Stockpiling and Network Modernization:

The joining of sustainable power sources into the electrical lattice has required progressions in energy capacity and matrix modernization. Energy capacity arrangements, including lithium-particle batteries and arising advancements like stream batteries, empower the effective stockpiling and recovery of power produced from renewables.

Lattice modernization endeavors include the arrangement of savvy network innovations that improve matrix unwavering quality, strength, and productivity. These advancements integrate constant checking, matrix mechanization, and request reaction abilities to upgrade energy dispersion.

The progress to decentralized energy age, where individual buyers can create and store their own power, is reshaping the conventional utility model. Microgrids, referenced prior, are a sign of this pattern, empowering confined energy age and utilization.

9.2 The contributions of other inventors and scientists in the field.

While illuminators like Thomas Edison and Nikola Tesla frequently take the spotlight in conversations of electrical designing and innovation, the historical backdrop of this field is packed with endless different creators and researchers who have made huge commitments. These uncelebrated yet truly great individuals have progressed how we might interpret power, created vital advancements, and made a permanent imprint on the cutting edge world. In this exposition, we will dig into the surprising commitments of a portion of these creators and researchers, revealing insight into their momentous work and persevering through influence.

1. **Michael Faraday: The Dad of Electromagnetism**

   Michael Faraday, an English physicist and scientific expert, is many times hailed as the dad of electromagnetism. His spearheading tests in the mid nineteenth century established the groundwork for how we might interpret electromagnetic enlistment and the standards behind electric engines and generators.

   Faraday's law of electromagnetic enlistment, figured out during the 1830s, states that a changing attractive field prompts an electromotive power (EMF) in a close by guide. This weighty disclosure prepared for the advancement of electric generators, which are at the center of current power age.

   Faraday's work likewise added to the comprehension of the connection among power and attraction, a basic idea that supports the activity of electric engines, transformers, and the whole field of electromechanical designing.

2. **Samuel Morse: The Message and Morse Code**

   Samuel Morse, an American creator and craftsman, is praised for his job in the improvement of the message and Morse code. During the 1830s and 1840s, Morse and his teammates fostered an electrical message framework that empowered significant distance correspondence utilizing coded electrical signs.

   The message reformed correspondence by permitting messages to be communicated quickly over significant stretches. It assumed a critical part in different areas, including news-casting, business, and transportation, empowering the quick trade of data.

   Morse code, a process for addressing letters and numbers utilizing groupings of dabs and runs, was contrived to work with productive correspondence by means of the message. Despite the fact that it was initially made for telecommunication, Morse code stays applicable today and is utilized in flight, sea correspondence, and beginner radio activities.

3. **James Agent Maxwell: The Unification of Power and Attraction**

   James Representative Maxwell, a Scottish physicist, made notable commitments to the unification of power and attraction through his plan of Maxwell's situations. During the nineteenth 100 years, Maxwell fostered a bunch of numerical conditions that depicted the way of behaving of electric and attractive fields.

   Maxwell's conditions laid out that electric and attractive fields are interrelated and that adjustments of one field can prompt changes in the other. This unification of electromagnetism made ready for the comprehension of electromagnetic waves, including the presence of light as an electromagnetic peculiarity.

   Maxwell's work had significant ramifications for the improvement of innovations like radio, TV, and remote correspondence. His conditions gave the hypothetical system to the transmission of electromagnetic transmissions and motivated creators like Guglielmo Marconi in the field of remote telecommunication.

4. **Heinrich Hertz: Trial Affirmation of Electromagnetic Waves**
   Heinrich Hertz, a German physicist, is known for his trial confirmation of Maxwell's electromagnetic wave hypothesis. In the late nineteenth 100 years, Hertz led a progression of examinations that exhibited the presence of electromagnetic waves, presently normally alluded to as radio waves.

   Hertz's investigations included producing and distinguishing electromagnetic waves utilizing flash holes and recieving wires. His work gave observational proof to the spread of electromagnetic waves at the speed of light and affirmed Maxwell's hypothetical expectations.

   The meaning of Hertz's tests couldn't possibly be more significant. They laid the foundation for the advancement of remote correspondence and the resulting creation of radio. Hertz's name is deified in the unit of recurrence, the hertz (Hz), used to gauge the cycles each second of electromagnetic waves.

5. **Alexander Graham Ringer: The Creation of the Phone**
   Alexander Graham Ringer, a Scottish-conceived designer and researcher, is most popular for his creation of the phone. In 1876, Ringer got the primary US patent for the phone, a gadget that changed significant distance correspondence by empowering the transmission of verbally expressed words over electrical wires.

   The phone reformed correspondence by permitting individuals to talk continuously, no matter what their actual distance. Ringer's innovation significantly affected society, trade, and industry, and it established the groundwork for the broadcast communications industry that keeps on developing today.

   Chime's work additionally stretched out to hearing impedance, and he devoted huge endeavors to creating advancements for the hard of hearing, including the innovation of the audiometer and the photophone.

6. **Charles Babbage: The Trailblazer of Software engineering**
   Charles Babbage, an English mathematician and creator, is in

many cases viewed as the trailblazer of software engineering. In the nineteenth hundred years, Babbage planned and conceptualized the "logical motor," a mechanical broadly useful PC.

The scientific motor was an earth shattering creation that consolidated key components of current processing, including a number juggling rationale unit, control course through contingent spreading and circling, and capacity as punched cards. Albeit the insightful motor was never completely worked during Babbage's lifetime because of mechanical impediments, its plan foreshadowed the standards of computerized calculation.

Babbage's work established the hypothetical starting point for present day PCs and motivated ensuing ages of PC researchers and specialists, including Alan Turing, who developed Babbage's thoughts and added to the improvement of the Turing machine, a hypothetical computational gadget.

7. **Robert Noyce and Jack Kilby: The Coordinated Circuit**

The improvement of the coordinated circuit (IC), a major part of present day hardware, owes a lot to crafted by Robert Noyce and Jack Kilby. In the last part of the 1950s and mid 1960s, these two specialists freely developed the coordinated circuit, a gadget that reformed the hardware business.

Noyce's and Kilby's creations killed the requirement for cumbersome and untrustworthy discrete parts by coordinating numerous electronic capabilities onto a solitary semiconductor chip. This leading edge made electronic gadgets more modest, more dependable, and more reasonable.

The coordinated circuit laid the preparation for the microelectronics insurgency, prompting the advancement of microchips, memory chips, and the quick scaling down of electronic gadgets. The cutting edge world, portrayed by cell phones, PCs, and innumerable electronic contraptions, is a demonstration of the groundbreaking force of the coordinated circuit.

8. **Tim Berners-Lee: The Internet**

   Sir Tim Berners-Lee, an English PC researcher, is the creator of the Internet (WWW). In the late twentieth 100 years, Berners-Lee proposed the idea of a hypertext framework that would permit data to be shared and gotten to universally through interconnected records.

   In 1990, he fostered the main web server and internet browser, denoting the introduction of the Internet. Berners-Lee's creation democratized data and correspondence, working with the trading of information, thoughts, and business on a worldwide scale.

   Today, the Internet is a necessary piece of present day life, and Berners-Lee's obligation to an open and decentralized web keeps on impacting the advancement of the web.

9. **Shinya Yamanaka and John Gurdon: Cell Reconstructing and Undifferentiated organisms**

   Shinya Yamanaka, a Japanese researcher, and John Gurdon, an English scientist, made historic commitments to the field of cell reinventing and immature microorganism research. In the mid 21st 100 years, Yamanaka and Gurdon freely found that experienced, particular cells could be reconstructed into a pluripotent state, likened to undeveloped immature microorganisms.

   Yamanaka's disclosure of prompted pluripotent undifferentiated cells (iPSCs) in 2006 opened new roads for regenerative medication and customized medical care. iPSCs can possibly produce patient-explicit cells for transplantation and illness displaying, offering expect treating conditions like Parkinson's infection, diabetes, and spinal line wounds.

   Gurdon's prior work on atomic transplantation in frogs, led during the 1960s, laid the preparation for Yamanaka's exploration and the ensuing improvement of iPSC innovation.

10. **Linus Torvalds: The Production of Linux**

Linus Torvalds, a Finnish computer programmer, is the maker of the Linux working framework piece. In 1991, Torvalds delivered the main form of Linux as an open-source project, welcoming coordinated effort from designers around the world.

Linux has since become quite possibly of the most broadly utilized working framework, fueling servers, supercomputers, implanted frameworks, and Android cell phones. Its open-source nature cultivates development and customization, and it plays had a urgent impact in the development of the open-source programming development.

Torvalds' commitments to the universe of programming significantly affect figuring, filling in as a model for cooperative turn of events and the democratization of innovation.

9.3 The ongoing evolution of electrical systems and their global impact.

The development of electrical frameworks has been a determined and groundbreaking excursion, set apart by ceaseless advancement and mechanical progressions. From the beginning of power bridled by pioneers like Thomas Edison and Nikola Tesla to the current period of brilliant matrices, environmentally friendly power, and zapped transportation, electrical frameworks have gone through significant changes. This paper investigates the continuous advancement of electrical frameworks and their worldwide effect, zeroing in on key turns of events, their importance, and the ramifications for society, the climate, and the worldwide economy.

1. **Shrewd Lattices: Preparing for Productive Energy The board** Savvy networks address a change in outlook in how power is created, sent, dispersed, and consumed. These high level electrical frameworks influence advanced innovation, sensors, and correspondence organizations to upgrade energy stream, improve unwavering quality, and empower constant checking and control. One of the essential targets of savvy matrices is to further develop energy productivity. By giving customers constant information

on their energy utilization and empowering two-way correspondence among utilities and end-clients, shrewd lattices engage people and associations to arrive at informed conclusions about energy utilization. This prompts diminished wastage, lower energy bills, and a more practical utilization of assets.

Also, savvy frameworks work with the combination of sustainable power sources, for example, sun based and wind, into the electrical matrix. They can naturally change power appropriation because of variances in sustainable power age, in this way improving matrix security and diminishing reliance on petroleum derivatives.

Universally, the reception of shrewd lattices is adding to a more practical and versatile energy framework. Nations like Germany, the US, and Japan have made significant interests in shrewd lattice innovation, expecting to diminish fossil fuel byproducts, further develop matrix unwavering quality, and upgrade energy security.

2. **Environmentally friendly power Reconciliation: A Progress to Clean Energy**

The continuous development of electrical frameworks is characteristically connected to the worldwide progress toward sustainable power sources. Sun based, wind, hydroelectric, and geothermal power are progressively becoming significant supporters of the world's power age blend.

Sustainable power coordination into electrical frameworks presents a few benefits. It, most importantly, decreases ozone depleting substance outflows and mitigates the natural effect of power age. Second, sustainable power sources are bountiful and can be tackled locally, lessening reliance on imported petroleum products and improving energy security. In conclusion, environmentally friendly power advancements keep on turning out to be more savvy, pursuing clean energy a serious decision in numerous districts.

China, for example, has arisen as a worldwide forerunner in

sustainable power organization, with monstrous interests in sun oriented and wind power. The country's aggressive focuses for carbon nonpartisanship and expanded dependence on clean energy feature the worldwide effect of environmentally friendly power mix.

3. **Jolted Transportation: The Shift to Electric Vehicles (EVs)**

The development of electrical frameworks stretches out to the domain of transportation, where the charge of vehicles is picking up speed. Electric vehicles (EVs) are turning out to be progressively famous because of their natural advantages, lower working expenses, and headways in battery innovation.

EVs are fueled by power put away in battery-powered batteries, which can be charged at home, at charging stations, or through quick charging organizations. This shift from gas powered motor vehicles to EVs has huge ramifications for diminishing fossil fuel byproducts and air contamination in metropolitan regions.

Countries all over the planet are setting aggressive focuses to transition away from conventional fuel and diesel vehicles. For instance, nations like Norway and the Netherlands have reported plans to boycott the offer of new petroleum derivative fueled vehicles by 2025 and 2030, separately. Moreover, significant automakers are focusing on creating a developing number of electric vehicles in their setups.

The worldwide effect of energized transportation stretches out past lessening ozone harming substance discharges. It additionally includes the advancement of charging foundation, lattice the board to oblige expanded power interest, and the potential for vehicle-to-network (V2G) innovation, permitting EVs to take care of overabundance energy back into the framework during top interest periods.

4. **Energy Capacity: The Way to Matrix Dependability and Renewables Reconciliation**

Energy capacity innovations assume a basic part in the continuous development of electrical frameworks. These frameworks store abundance power when age surpasses request and delivery it while required, upgrading network dependability, and empowering more prominent combination of discontinuous sustainable power sources.

Battery energy capacity frameworks (BESS) have acquired noticeable quality, thanks to some degree to headways in lithium-particle battery innovation. BESS can store power from sustainable sources like breeze and sun based for sometime in the future, giving a consistent stockpile of force in any event, when the sun isn't sparkling or the breeze isn't blowing.

The meaning of energy stockpiling is exemplified by projects like the Hornsdale Power Save in South Australia, one of the biggest lithium-particle battery establishments on the planet. This office has effectively settled the local network, answering vacillations in energy organic market inside milliseconds.

Moreover, energy capacity is a basic part of microgrids, which are limited energy frameworks fit for working freely from the fundamental lattice. Microgrids give versatility during lattice interruptions and empower networks to depend on nearby energy age.

5. Web of Things (IoT) Incorporation: Upgrading Proficiency and Dependability

The combination of the Web of Things (IoT) into electrical frameworks is introducing another period of availability and information driven independent direction. IoT gadgets, outfitted with sensors and correspondence capacities, can gather and send constant information on different parts of electrical framework, from matrix execution to hardware wellbeing.

For instance, IoT sensors can screen the state of electrical cables, transformers, and substations, recognizing issues, for example, overheating or gear disappointments before they lead to blackouts. This proactive support diminishes margin time, further develops framework unwavering quality, and broadens the life expectancy of electrical resources.

Moreover, IoT-empowered request reaction programs permit utilities to speak with end-clients and change power utilization during top interest periods. By boosting buyers to diminish their energy use when the matrix is anxious, IoT mix can forestall power outages, lessen the requirement for expensive foundation redesigns, and lower power costs for shoppers.

6. **Decentralized Energy Age: Enabling Prosumers**

The continuous development of electrical frameworks is set apart by a shift toward decentralized energy age. This pattern empowers individual buyers, frequently alluded to as prosumers, to create their own power through housetop sunlight based chargers, little wind turbines, or other sustainable power sources.

Prosumers can take care of overabundance energy back into the lattice, acquiring credits or remuneration for their commitments. This two-way progression of power obscures the lines among buyers and makers, democratizing energy age and conveyance.

Germany's Energiewende (energy change) is a prominent illustration of decentralized energy age's worldwide effect. The nation's strategies and motivators have prompted a critical expansion in environmentally friendly power establishments and a shift toward privately created power. Comparative patterns are arising in different nations, cultivating energy freedom and local area flexibility.

7. **Jolt of Ventures: Supportable Assembling**

Jolt is likewise changing modern areas, including assembling and weighty industry. Charged modern cycles, controlled by clean power, offer a more economical option in contrast to customary petroleum derivative based tasks.

For instance, electric circular segment heaters (EAFs) are utilized in steelmaking and can be controlled by power created from sustainable sources. The reception of EAFs decreases fossil fuel byproducts in the steel business, an area known for its critical natural impression.

Besides, jolt of transportation inside modern offices, like the utilization of electric forklifts and trucks, adds to bring down discharges and further developed air quality inside modern premises.

8. **Worldwide Effect and Natural Ramifications**

The continuous advancement of electrical frameworks conveys critical worldwide ramifications, especially with regards to ecological maintainability and environmental

change alleviation. Electrical frameworks play a focal part to play in lessening ozone harming substance emanations and changing to a low-carbon energy future.

The reconciliation of environmentally friendly power sources into electrical lattices lessens dependence on petroleum products, in this manner controling fossil fuel byproducts from power age. Zapped transportation, particularly when EVs are accused of clean energy, diminishes discharges from the transportation area, which is a significant supporter of air contamination and fossil fuel byproducts.

Moreover, the utilization of energy stockpiling frameworks improves matrix dependability and can decrease the requirement for reinforcement power sources that depend on petroleum products. This adds to a stronger electrical framework equipped for enduring outrageous climate occasions and cataclysmic events.

Nonetheless, the natural effect of the continuous development of electrical frameworks isn't without challenges. The creation and removal of lithium-particle batteries, a basic part of numerous cutting edge electrical applications, raise worries about asset extraction, reusing, and squander the board.

Moreover, the development of sustainable power foundation, like sun based homesteads and wind turbines, can have ecological and land-use suggestions. Cautious preparation and manageable practices are fundamental to relieve these effects and guarantee the drawn out manageability of clean energy advances.

9. **Financial Ramifications: Occupation Creation and Monetary Development**

The continuous development of electrical frameworks has critical financial ramifications, including position creation and monetary development. The shift toward sustainable power, energized transportation, and savvy framework advancements has prompted the development of new ventures and business open doors.

The sustainable power area, specifically, has seen significant work development. As per the Worldwide Environmentally friendly power Office (IRENA), the worldwide environmentally friendly power labor force arrived at 11.5 million positions in 2019. This pattern is supposed to go on as nations put resources into clean energy innovations and endeavor to meet their environment objectives.

Also, the turn of events and arrangement of electrical frameworks innovations, like high level sensors, energy capacity arrangements, and IoT gadgets, set out open doors for development and business venture. New businesses and laid out organizations the same are driving mechanical progressions and financial improvement in this area.

10. **Mechanical Difficulties and the Requirement for Development**

The continuous development of electrical frameworks additionally presents mechanical difficulties that require consistent advancement and examination. One such test is the discontinuity of sustainable power sources. Sun oriented and wind power age can fluctuate contingent upon weather patterns and season of day, requiring energy stockpiling arrangements and lattice the executives procedures to supply guarantee a steady power.

Moreover, the zap of transportation presents difficulties connected with charging foundation, battery innovation, and framework limit. As the reception of EVs keeps on developing, addressing these difficulties is essential to oblige expanded power interest and empower consistent charging encounters for purchasers.

Online protection is one more area of concern, given the rising availability and digitization of electrical frameworks. Shielding basic foundation from cyberattacks and guaranteeing the protection and security of IoT gadgets and brilliant networks are central.

Advancement is critical to tending to these difficulties. Investigation into cutting edge materials for energy capacity, lattice the board calculations, and online protection arrangements is fundamental for drive the continuous advancement of electrical frameworks.